AP'

The Restless Sea

OCEAN WILDLIFE

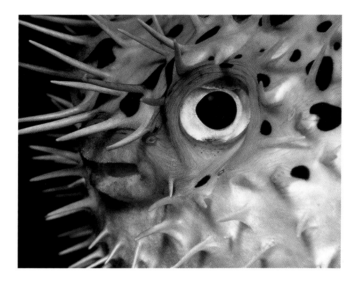

CAROLE GARBUNY VOGEL

Franklin Watts®

A Division of Scholastic Inc.
New York • Toronto • London • Auckland • Sydney
Mexico City • New Delhi • Hong Kong
Danbury, Connecticut

FOR DR. JOAN EIGER GOTTLIEB,
who taught me biology in high school and was the most inspiring teacher I ever had

ACKNOWLEDGMENTS

Many thanks to Professor Peter Guth, Oceanography Department, U.S. Naval Academy, Annapolis, Maryland, who took time from his busy schedule to read and critique the manuscript, and answer my many questions. His vast knowledge of the field and keen insight were reflected in his comments.

I am indebted to editorial researcher Kathleen Derzipilski, San Diego, California, for a superb job of fact checking.

It was a thrill and an honor to have my former high school biology teacher, Joan Eiger Gottlieb, Ph.D., Pittsburgh, Pennsylvania, read the manuscript for accuracy and after making several minor corrections, tell me that I passed with flying colors.

I am grateful to fellow writer, Dr. Joyce A. Nettleton, Denver, Colorado, for her invaluable criticism, scientific expertise, and sense of humor. Special thanks to students Stephen, Daniel, and Joanna Guth for reading the manuscript from the kid perspective.

My sincere appreciation to my husband, Mark A. Vogel, for the encouragement and understanding that has become his hallmark. I would also like to acknowledge the help of the many other people who helped either directly or indirectly.

Finally, my heartfelt thanks to my editor, Kate Nunn, for having faith in my writing ability and the talent to turn my manuscripts into spectacular books.

Photographs © 2003: Animals Animals: 41 (C. Milkins/OSF), 64 (D. Shale/OSF); Corbis Images: 85 (D. Robert & Lorri Franz), 77 (Raymond Gehman), 86 (Martin Harvey/Gallo Images), cover (Charles Krebs Photography), 82, 83 (Pat O'Hara), 70, 71 (Craig Tuttle); Dembinsky Photo Assoc./Mark J. Thomas: 16; Photo Researchers, NY/Biophoto Associates: 26 left; Seapics.com: 30 (Brandon D. Cole), 12, 38, 39, 61, 66, 67 (Mark Conlin), 32 (Bob Cranston), 36 (Florian Graner), 15, 78 (Richard Herrmann), 43 (Yoshi Hirata), 40 (Steven Kazlowski), 44 (Rudie Kuiter), 52 (A & C Mahaney), 26 right, 27 (Peter Parks/iq3-d), 10, 11, 21, 46, 47, 48, 49, 55, 80, 81 (Doug Perrine), 13, 69 (D.R. & T.L. Schrichte), 7 (John G. Shedd Aquarium/Patrice Ceisel), 57 (Mark Strickland), 1, 62, 63 (Masa Ushioda), 4 (Ingrid Visser), 8, 18 (James D. Watt), 28, 29 (Doc White), 72, 73 (David Wrobel); Stone/Getty Images/Darryl Torckler: 34, 35; Taxi/Getty Images: 25 (Georgette Douwma), 58 (Herwarth Voightmann); The Image Bank/Getty Images: 75 (Steve Satushek), 23 (Joshua Singer).

Book design by Marie O'Neill

Library of Congress Cataloging-in-Publication Data

Vogel, Carole Garbuny.
    Ocean wildlife / Carole G. Vogel.
        p. cm. — (The restless sea)
Summary: Discusses how various underwater creatures have adapted to their environment in order to keep themselves safe from dangerous predators.
    ISBN 0-531-12324-3 (lib. Bdg.)   0-531-16681 (pbk.)
1. Marine animals—Juvenile literature. [1. Marine animals. 2. Predatory animals.] I. Title.
    QL122.2.V64 2003
    591.77—dc21
        2003005302

contents

chapter 1

SEA CHALLENGES

In 1996 Martin Richardson was aboard a boat in the Middle East's Gulf of Aqaba, when the crew spotted five dolphins. The captain stopped the craft so Richardson and two others could swim alongside the animals. After a quick dip with the dolphins, Richardson's companions returned to the boat, but Richardson decided to spend more time with the pod (group). To his disappointment, the dolphins soon departed, leaving Richardson alone in the water.

Suddenly, a huge shark streaked up from the depths and attacked Richardson, biting deeply into his back, chest, and shoulder. Although Richardson fought back he could not prevail against the hungry meat eater. Just as it appeared that all was lost, three of the dolphins raced back to Richardson's rescue. They circled the wounded man and slapped their tail flukes and flippers on the water's surface to scare away the shark. As the predator retreated, one of Richardson's companions pulled him from the water. The crew administered first aid to control the massive bleeding. He was taken to an Egyptian hospital, where the life-threatening wounds were treated. Without the intervention of the dolphins and his friends, Richardson surely would have died.

There are many other true-life tales of helpful dolphins rescuing humans or guiding ships safely through treacherous waters. Movies, TV programs, and aquarium shows focus on the sociable nature of trained dolphins. Every year, thousands of people pay tour operators for the privilege of communing with dolphins in captivity or in the wild. Even the fixed smile on the faces of many dolphin species lends credence to the myth that all dolphins are friendly creatures.

Yet, dolphins can also exhibit a nasty side. They have been known to bite, ram, and pull people underwater. Some dolphins are ruthless killers. They use their beaks and sharp teeth to batter and slash porpoises, their smaller

Dolphins are small toothed whales.

"cousins." These killings appear unrelated to hunger, as the dolphins do not eat the dead porpoises. Perhaps porpoises sometimes compete with dolphins for territory.

Some dolphins pose a danger to the young of their own kind. Scientists have witnessed bottle-nosed dolphins bashing baby dolphins and butting them into the air. The scientists theorize that the killers are males disposing of the offspring of rivals. A few days after a young dolphin perishes, its mother becomes available for mating and starting a new family.

FIT FOR LIFE IN THE SEA

The dolphin is only one of a myriad of different kinds of wild animals that live in the ocean. People tend to give these creatures human traits and measure their behaviors by human standards without understanding the reality of ocean life. Unlike humans, few sea creatures die of old age. Most end up in the belly of a hungry predator. Adaptations—specialized body parts and behavior patterns—help the animals find food, attract mates, and avoid being eaten.

Living in a water world provides different challenges than living on solid ground. In the open ocean, far from land, few hiding places can be found. Waves, tides, and currents tug on the ocean, keeping it in continual motion. A sea creature must expend more energy to stay in one place than if it simply drifted with the flow.

During the day, sunlight penetrates the water to a depth of about 650 feet (200 meters). Beneath that lies a dim world where scant sunlight reaches. Below 3,300 feet (1,000 meters) or so, everything is bathed in darkness. Three-fourths of the ocean, the largest habitat on the planet, is pitch-black. Sight, the sense that humans rely on most, is nearly worthless in these sunless waters. Even where sunlight illuminates the sea, few landmarks exist to serve as signs to point the way. And in most places visibility extends no more than 100 feet (300 meters) because of the murkiness. Typically, visual conditions are so poor that most large whales can't see their own tails. To you it would be like living in a thick fog.

Bioluminescence

In the twilight world between 650 feet (200 meters) and 3,300 feet (1,000 meters) many animals create their own light, like fireflies. In a process called bioluminescence, chemicals inside specialized cells react to produce light energy. Animals use bioluminescence to confuse predators, lure prey, and entice mates. Some animals have large numbers of these bioluminescent cells clustered together as light-producing organs that generate a glow. Others house colonies of bioluminescent bacteria in their tissues to do the job.

Flashlight fish have luminous patches beneath their eyes. They can blink the lights on and off.

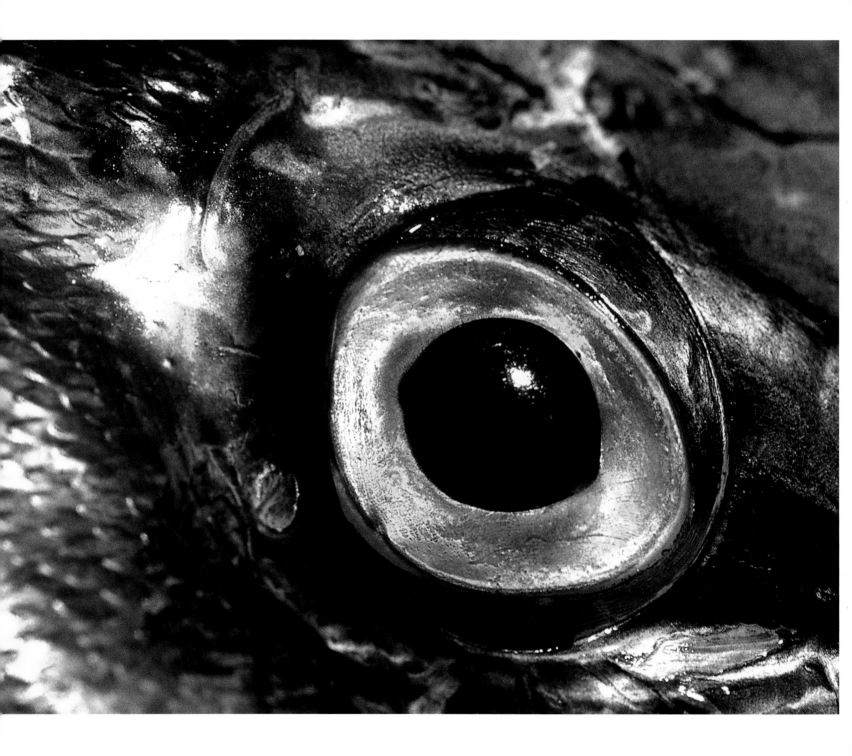

Sensing the Sea

Fish are one of the most successful animals in the ocean, with about 16,000 marine species. The eyes of most fish are well suited to make the best of low-light conditions. They are more sensitive to light than human eyes. And they lack eyelids because there is no need to shield them from bright light. Typically, fish eyes are spaced far apart, giving fish the ability to see to the left and right simultaneously and to detect predators approaching from behind.

Other specialized senses—some quite different from those of humans— help fish and other sea creatures monitor and respond to their environment. The water itself provides cues. Water pressure and saltiness increase with depth but the temperature decreases. As a result, the ocean consists of different levels, like a layer cake, each with a distinct pressure, temperature, and salinity, which animals can detect. Although each layer varies only slightly from the one above or below it, the layers usually remain separate. Seawater can flow horizontally for thousands of miles within a layer without mixing with neighboring ones.

Currents—"rivers"—in the sea, carry water over great distances in fairly predictable paths. Currents may be hot or cold. Some scoot across the surface, while others snake along the ocean floor. Still others rise up from the chilly depths or sink down into them.

The odor of water varies from place to place. Chemicals emitted by rocks and sediments, the odors given off by animals, the scent of animal wastes, and the breakdown products of rotting organisms give water a specific character. Many sea animals have a sharp sense of smell and can detect minute regional differences in odors. Odors not only provide information about location, but can also alert animals to predators looming near or the position of prey. Sharks are especially attuned to the scent of blood.

Map Sense

Sea turtles may migrate thousands of miles between their breeding grounds and feeding grounds. Perhaps the longest and most complex journeys are taken by

This is the eye of a mahimahi, also known as a dolphin fish.

loggerhead turtles. Shortly after hatching, baby loggerheads leave their nests on tropical sandy beaches and scurry into the ocean. Most do not succeed. The hatchlings, about the size of a child's hand, make tasty snacks for waiting gulls, raccoons, and crabs. Near shore, the waters bring little respite since sharks and other carnivorous fish also have an appetite for baby turtles. Survival for the babies depends on reaching deep water. As few as 1 in 1,000 hatchlings live to adulthood.

Baby loggerheads born on the beaches of eastern Florida instinctively seek out the Gulf Stream, a fast-moving, warm current that sweeps alongside the east coast of the United States. The Gulf Stream is part of the 8,000-mile (13,000-kilometer) North Atlantic Gyre, a gigantic "wheel" of water that loops around the North Atlantic Ocean. The loggerheads migrate within the gyre and find food along its plankton-rich edges. Their trek may last up to 10 years. Females return to the very beaches where they were hatched to lay their own eggs.

How turtles find their way across the featureless ocean realm has long puzzled scientists. But now it appears that these animals are born with the ability to "read" Earth's magnetic field like a road map. The "map" tells them where they are and where they want to go. Their bodies contain magnetite, crystals of magnetic iron ore that react like a compass. The "compass" helps a turtle know when to change direction. Turtles may also be able to orient themselves by swell patterns and the direction of waves. (Swells are a series of smooth-topped waves that look like rolling mounds.)

In the open ocean, a clump of sargassum seaweed provides a hiding place for a recently hatched loggerhead turtle.

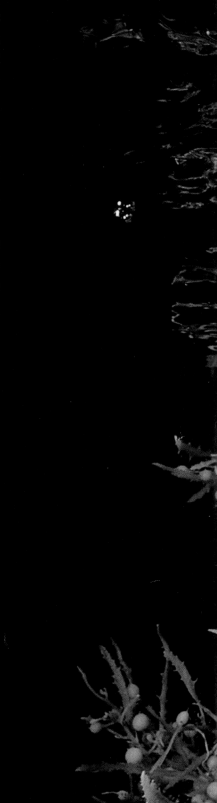

animals have directional sense.

12

Most sockeye salmon are four years old when they return to their home streams to spawn and die.

Salmon appear to have the same magnetic map sense as turtles. In addition, they use their sense of smell to navigate. Salmon begin their lives in clear mountain streams. When they are a year old, they journey downstream to the ocean. There they live for several years, feasting on the bounty of the sea. After they mature, the salmon respond to an urge to return to their home stream and spawn—reproduce. Their sense of smell helps them find the place where they were born. Dissolved chemicals in the water give each river and stream its own distinctive odor.

Magnet Earth

Earth is an enormous bar magnet. Its magnetic field is strongest at the magnetic poles, which lie near the geographic North and South Poles. You can observe the effects of the magnetic field with a compass. The compass needle's north-seeking end will turn toward Earth's magnetic north.

SOUND PICTURES

Sound waves carry well in water, so many marine creatures use sound instead of light to picture their surroundings. Sound waves are vibrations produced when an object moves. The vibrations rush away from the source just as waves ripple outward when you plunk a stone in water. In humans, the outer ear collects sound waves and funnels them to the inner ear. There the vibrations are translated into nerve impulses and sent to the hearing center in the brain to be interpreted. Fish lack external ears, but sound vibrations travel easily through their bodies to their inner ears.

Fish also detect vibrations with their lateral line sense—a cross between hearing and touch. A lateral line consists of a series of fluid-filled tubes arranged in a line

Can you find the lateral line of this giant trevally? (Hint: look at the base of the tail.)

13

beneath the skin. There is one lateral line on each side of a fish. Lateral lines detect vibrations in the water as waves of pressure. They allow a fish to sense the direction of water movement, maintain position in a school, and find prey nearby. Lateral lines provide excellent short-range detection, but for long-range detection fish rely on hearing.

Schooling: Safety in Numbers

A school is a large group of fish that swims at the same speed and in the same direction. Some kinds of fish, such as herring, flock together in the millions. Although there is no definite leader, schooling fish move in unison like well-rehearsed dancers. Swerving, twisting, flitting, even stopping, they maintain a uniform space between individuals. Fish have a better chance of dodging predators in a school than they do as individuals. When an intruder nears, the fish may scatter in different directions, confusing the predator, or the school may break in two and simply swim around it. Some fish may perish but most members of the school will live.

Dolphins have an even more sophisticated way of utilizing vibrations to detect objects and orient themselves. The animals emit sound waves, usually high-frequency clicks. The sound waves zip through the water, bounce off the target, and return as echoes. The farther away an object is, the more time it takes for the echo to return. Known as echolocation, this use of sound waves is much like focusing a flashlight beam on an object. Instead of light bouncing back and sending a visual image to the eyes, however, it is sound that bounces back. It travels through the dolphin's lower jaw, and produces vibrations in the inner ear. The animal processes the information to pinpoint the size, shape, and distance of objects.

Dolphins use high-pitched chirps and whistles to communicate with other dolphins in the same vicinity but not those far away. High-frequency sounds cannot be sent over long distances because they fade out rapidly.

Blue whales and fin whales have overcome the problem of long-distance transmission. They produce loud, low-pitched booms that travel hundreds of miles. These rumblings probably alert other members of their species to rich feeding

Anchovies are "fast food" for blue sharks.

To attract a mate, this male humpback whale "sings" the same song over and over.

grounds and help whales find mates. Blue whales and fin whales also make use of a strange phenomenon called the deep sound channel. At a depth of approximately 3,300 feet (1,000 meters), the salinity, temperature, and pressure of the water create a layer that traps sound waves. This channel can carry sound waves more than 11,000 miles (18,000 kilometers). Some whale experts believe that blue whales and fin whales may employ this channel to communicate with each other across an entire ocean basin. The whales may also use echoes from these ocean-crossing booms to chart a path across the sea.

Unlike humans, whales lack vocal cords. They probably create their sounds by moving air within the spaces of their heads. Male humpback whales produce some of the most complex sounds. They "sing" to attract females. Head down with flippers stretched out, the males moan, groan, click, whistle, chirp, and yup. The songs—intricate patterns of sounds—can last 2 to 30 minutes and may be repeated for hours on end. While the melodies sound eerie and haunting to human ears, to a female humpback they say, "Choose me over the other guys!"

The Electric Sense

The muscle movements of animals give off minute amounts of electricity. Some of the electric current seeps out and travels readily through water. All sharks and rays—fish that look like flattened sharks with wings—can sense these faint electric currents. Electric receptors in their skin are so sensitive they can even detect the electricity produced by a beating heart. Sharks and rays depend on their electric sense for defense and to find food. Occasionally sharks swallow aluminum cans and license plates. Saltwater is a good conductor of the weak current these metal objects generate, and sharks may mistake them for a nutritious treat. Humans never developed electric receptors. The sensation sharks and rays experience is different from the pain you feel if electricity zaps you.

Some species of rays not only detect electrical charges, they can produce them too. These rays have batterylike electric organs on both sides of their head. The animals can voluntarily turn the organs on and off. Living cells capable of generating electricity comprise the battery. Rays can deliver an electric jolt strong enough to stun their prey before eating it. About 450 different species of rays live in the ocean, but only 38 kinds are known to deliver a shock.

Electric eels, which make their homes in South American rivers, are the kings of shock. They are not even true eels but relatives of catfish. An electric eel can produce a 600-volt shock, enough to stun a horse.

chapter 2

EAT AND BE EATEN

After midnight on July 30, 1945, a Japanese submarine in the South Pacific Ocean torpedoed the American battle cruiser USS *Indianapolis.* This was one of the last sneak attacks of World War II. Within 12 minutes the ship sank, taking about 300 sailors with it. Another 900 men wound up in shark-inhabited waters, most without lifeboats, food, or water. In the terrifying darkness the survivors searched for debris to which they could cling. Some had escaped with life jackets. Others were not as fortunate. The men tried to cluster in large groups for safety. During the long night, the waves and current dispersed the groups over a wide area. In the hours before dawn, about 100 sailors who had been injured when the ship exploded died from their wounds. The rest clung to the hope that they would soon be rescued. However, the explosion had disabled the ship's communication system, and no distress signal had gone out.

The first sharks arrived after daylight. They swam near the survivors and brushed against their limbs but did not bite. By day two, however, more sharks appeared. More of the wounded had succumbed to their injuries, and additional men had died from thirst or from drinking seawater. The sharks began to feast on the dead. Occasionally, men became delirious, broke away from their groups, and became easy pickings for the sharks.

By day three, the sharks grew bolder. Stalking their prey, they circled the groups from below. Horrified, the men tried to protect themselves. Some curled up to appear as small as possible. Others thrashed and pounded the water to scare away the predators. Still others hung motionless in the water. Sometimes the strategies succeeded, other times they failed. . . . Death came quickly to those unfortunate men selected by the sharks.

This great white shark is ready for a meal.

The U.S. Navy never noticed that the *Indianapolis* was missing, so no search and rescue operation was launched. By the fourth day, when a passing plane happened to spot the survivors, fewer than half the men were still alive. In the end, only 320 men were plucked from the sea, 4 of whom died shortly afterward.

Grisly as the feeding frenzy was, the man-eating sharks were not cold, calculating murderers. They were wild animals, doing what hungry creatures do. They took advantage of a new food source in their territory.

About 375 species of sharks exist, but the vast majority of them are harmless to humans. The three kinds that pose the greatest danger to people are great white sharks, tiger sharks, and bull sharks. Approximately 70 to 100 shark attacks on humans occur annually worldwide, with perhaps 5 to 15 deaths resulting. This is strikingly low considering that millions of people swim in the ocean and participate in water sports every year. In fact if you are a beachgoer, you are more likely be killed driving back and forth to the shore than you are from a shark assault in the water.

Sharks have more to fear from humans than humans from sharks. Fishers kill about 100 million sharks each year to meet the demand for shark fin soup in the Far East. In Hong Kong a single bowl of this delicacy commands as much as $100.

KINDS OF FISH

Sharks, along with rays, belong to a class of fish known as cartilaginous fishes. They don't have a single bone in their bodies. Their lightweight skeletons consist of cartilage, the same kind of flexible tissue that supports your nose and ears. Most other kinds of fish have heavier skeletons made mainly of bone. They are classified as bony fishes. Pointy, toothlike structures are in the skin of cartilaginous fishes, giving it the texture or feel of sandpaper. Overlapping scales coated with mucous cover the bodies of most bony fishes and give them a slimy surface. Nearly all fish are cold-blooded—their body temperature is about the same as that of the surrounding water. The exceptions are marlin, certain tuna, and great white sharks, which can raise their body temperature. This increases their speed and ability to chase prey.

Fish "breathe" through gills. These are structures on each side of the head

Like most bony fish, this short bigeye has an outer covering of thin overlapping scales.

that remove dissolved oxygen from the water and release carbon dioxide. Fish gulp in water through their open mouths and push it out through the gills. In bony fish, a hard flap covers the gills. The flap moves back and forth, constantly pumping water and ensuring an adequate supply of oxygen-rich water to the gills. Sharks and other cartilaginous fish lack this flap so they must swim continually, even when sleeping, to produce a steady flow over their gills.

Although fishes vary greatly in size and shape, most have the same general form. Typically, fish have a streamlined body—the head and tail are smaller and more tapered than the bulk of the body. This makes it easier for fish to push water aside while swimming. Most fish propel themselves through water by undulating the entire body. Some fish swing their powerful tails, and others move only their fins. Fins aid in steering, balance, and braking. Fish come equipped with two sets of paired fins. They also have several solitary fins on their back, underside, and tail that provide added stability.

Fish are more dense than water and thus have a tendency to sink. To counteract this, the majority of bony fishes possess a swim bladder. This internal, balloonlike organ expands or contracts to regulate the amount of gas inside the fish. That in turn helps the fish stay afloat at different depths. Cartilaginous fish don't have a swim bladder so they must swim to keep from sinking.

In addition to the cartilaginous and bony fishes, there is a third and much smaller class of fish: jawless fishes. Jawless fish form skeletons made of cartilage but they lack jaws to open and close their mouths. Unable to bite, these fish have mouthpart adaptations and vicous behaviors that allow them to stab, scrape, or suck in their food.

The typical bony fish is oval shaped. As a bony fish grows older, its scales get bigger. Unlike humans, nearly all fish continue to grow throughout their lives. Growth rings on the scales reveal the fish's age in the same way as the rings of a tree trunk show a tree's age.

Sharks are the most numerous of the cartilaginous fish. The mouths of most sharks are filled with row after row of long, pointed, curved teeth. When teeth in the front row break or fall out, other teeth shift forward as replacements. A

A sand tiger shark always swims with its mouth open. Its many fanglike teeth give this shark a truly menacing appearance.

shark's teeth are good for tearing and cutting, but a shark cannot chew. It must grasp its prey in its teeth and rapidly twist its body to gouge out large chunks.

Another kind of cartilaginous fish—the rays—have wide, flat bodies with powerful fins that resemble wings. Manta rays, the most majestic of the rays, may attain a "wingspan" of 20 feet (6 meters) and weigh as much as two tons. Using their mouths as strainers, mantas sift tiny fishes and crustaceans from the water.

With their "wings," stingrays scoop up sediments on the seafloor in pursuit of clams, oysters, and other shellfish. They crush their prey with their powerful jaws to break open the shells. Most stingrays possess whiplike tails with venomous stingers that they wield for defensive purposes.

Lampreys are jawless fish. Vampirelike, they latch onto another fish with their mouths. Using their sharp teeth, they puncture the skin of their victim and then suck the blood and body fluids.

Hagfish are bottom-dwelling jawless fish. Eyeless, they make their living as scavengers, targeting dead or dying fish. They enter their prey through the gills, mouth, or anus and burrow through the body devouring the flesh.

Links in the Chain of Life and Death

All organisms require energy to live, grow, and reproduce. In most ecosystems, energy enters in the form of sunlight. Producers—plants, algae, and some bacteria—capture energy from sunlight and use it to make their own food from carbon dioxide and water. This process is called photosynthesis. Animals cannot make their own food energy so they must consume the producers or other animals. When a consumer feasts on a producer, some of the food energy passes to the consumer. If a consumer falls prey to another consumer, food energy is transferred again. Some animals, such as lobsters, are scavengers. They nibble on the carcasses of dead organisms to gain their energy. Decomposers—certain bacteria and fungi—ultimately triumph over even the largest creatures. They break down the droppings and the dead bodies of all organisms, and return the raw materials to the environment.

Food chains typically describe the feeding relationships within an ecosystem. But they also depict a trail of death. Most ocean food chains begin with

The mouth of a
southern stingray is
located on its
underside. When
this stingray hunts, it
spreads out on sand
or soft mud on the
seafloor and digs for
crabs, fish, and clams.
Its jaws are strong
enough to crush the
hard shells of clams
like a nutcracker.

phytoplankton—tiny bacteria or one-celled algae that float on the surface. Phytoplankton are the producers and require sunlight to do their photosynthetic magic. Since bright sunlight reaches only the topmost layer of the ocean, phytoplankton must live at the "roof of the ocean." They stay adrift in the sea at the mercy of wind, waves, and currents. Without the energy-trapping phytoplankton—the first link in most marine food chains—the magnificent multitude of sea creatures would disappear.

Diatoms

Diatoms, which predominate in cold water, and dinoflagellates, which flourish in warm water, are the most abundant kinds of algae in the ocean. Like all phytoplankton, they grow and reproduce rapidly. However, the availability of nitrogen, phosphorus, iron, and other mineral nutrients in the water limit their growth.

A dinoflagellate

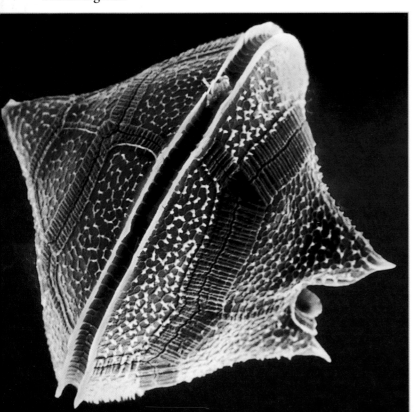

Zooplankton are tiny floating animals, such as shellfish larvae, tiny fish, and copepods. Zooplankton feed on phytoplankton and are in turn preyed upon by larger animals. Some zooplankton have developed a strategy that decreases their chances of being snatched by bigger, sight-dependent animals. During daylight these zooplankton journey down into the dimly lit depth to escape detection. At night they rise to the surface to feast on phytoplankton. The zooplankton may travel as much as 1,300 feet (400 meters) each way. When you consider their microscopic

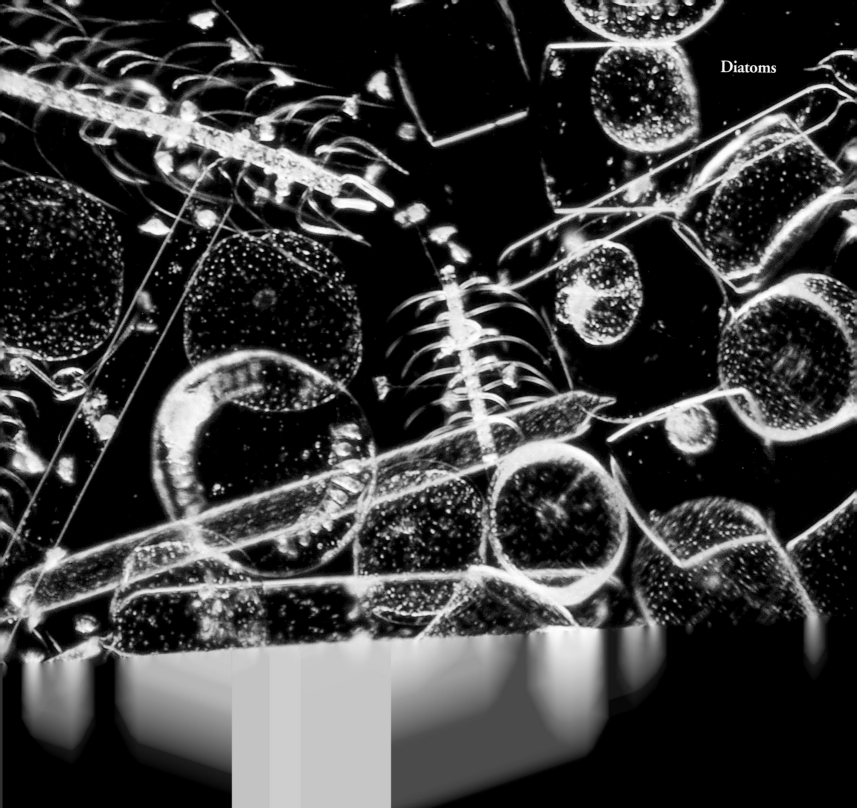

Diatoms

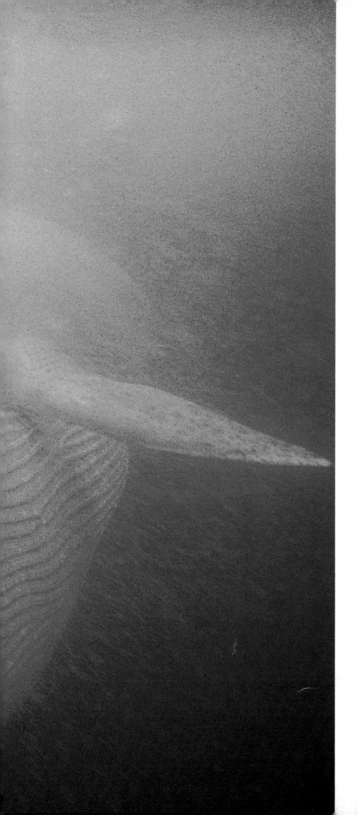

size, their daily trip is equivalent to a person scaling a 25-mile-high (40-kilometer) ladder each dawn and then climbing back down at dusk.

Small fish, such as herring, scarf down zooplankton, and become the third link in the chain. The small fish, in turn, are consumed by large fish, such as bluefish. And the large fish may be eaten by an even larger fish or mammal.

Ironically, the giants of the sea—baleen whales—depend on the smallest creatures for food. Instead of teeth, baleen whales have long, thin baleen plates that hang from their upper jaws like teeth on a comb. These plates consist of the same material as fingernails. The outer edges are smooth, but the inner edges split into a bristly fringe that meshes together to create a filter, similar to a sieve. When a baleen whale eats, it allows water and prey to pour into its mouth. The whale then snaps it jaws shut but leaves its "lips" slightly open. The whale forces the water out through the baleen, trapping tiny prey inside its mouth. During feeding, long parallel folds under the whale's throat may stretch open, allowing the mouth to expand and the whale to consume more food.

Blue whales are the largest animals on Earth, with the potential to reach a length of 110 feet (34 m). They feed on krill, small shrimplike animals that vary in length from less than 1/2 inch (1 cm) to 2 1/2 inches (6 cm).

Another group of whales, the toothed whales, have sharp teeth as opposed to baleen. Dolphins, porpoises, sperm whales, and killer whales are toothed whales. They seize fish or squid one at a time and swallow them headfirst.

Whales can dive deeply and stay underwater for long periods of time. They are mammals so they must rise to the surface to breathe air. Baleen whales breathe through paired blowholes—modified nostrils—on their backs. Toothed whales have a single blowhole. With each breath, a whale creates a spout, a fine mist that sprays up into the air. To propel themselves through water, whales pump their flukes—flattened tail flippers—up and down. Paddlelike flippers help them steer and maintain balance. Whales are warm-blooded: their bodies maintain a constant temperature that is about the same as humans. A thick layer of blubber beneath the skin insulates a whale from the cold and can be broken down to provide energy when food is unavailable.

Wrong-Way Humphrey

In 1985 a humpback whale wandered into San Francisco Bay and began to journey up the Sacramento River. Nicknamed Humphrey, the Wrong-way Whale, the bus-sized mammal swam inland more than 60 miles (100 kilometers) from the ocean. Along the way he attracted considerable attention. The whale-loving public worried that the lost whale could not find its way back. Marine biologists feared that prolonged exposure to freshwater was weakening the animal. Government officials were afraid that Humphrey would ground himself in a shallow channel. If he died, how could they ever dispose of his 38-ton body before it began to rot and stink?

More than three weeks after the whale trek began, rescue workers lured Humphrey back to the sea. Through underwater speakers pulled by a boat, they broadcast a special call humpbacks trumpet while feeding as a group. This call to chow down worked like a dinner bell. Humphrey trailed the boat and soon returned to the sea to live out his natural life.

A humpback whale with a mouth full of prey and seawater

Whale Falls

The corpse of a whale that dies in the open ocean sinks to the bottom. Scientists call this a "whale fall." Over the deepest part of the sea, the carcasses of fallen whales plunge nearly 7 miles (11 kilometers) to their final resting place.

If bottom dwellers could party, a whale fall would be a cause of great jubilation. Scavengers, such as crabs, sharks, and hagfish, arrive at the corpse first. They devour most of the soft tissue, taking up to 6 months to strip a good-sized carcass to the bone. Then furry polychaete worms take over for about a year. Swarming over the giant skeleton, they cover the bones like an ugly shag carpet, consuming leftover tidbits.

The bones, rich in fats and oils, provide a decades-long meal for an army of decay bacteria. During the decay process these bacteria release sulfides—sulfur-containing compounds. The sulfides then attract sulfur-loving bacteria, which grow in thick white and yellow mats over the skeleton. Worms, mollusks, clams, and other invertebrates graze on the bacteria. In one study, investigators counted more than 30,000 organisms, representing more than 200 species, feasting on a single whale skeleton.

The Underwater Landscape

The basin of the world ocean is too small to hold all the ocean's water. The overflow spills onto the continental shelf, the gently sloping land edging the continents. The water above the shelf is relatively shallow—rarely exceeding a depth of 650 feet (200 meters). It supports the majority of the sea creatures that humans eat. A steep underwater cliff—the continental slope—separates the shelf from the abyssal plain on the deep-ocean floor. The slope plummets about 13,000 feet (4,000 meters) before leveling off.

The abyssal plain is the flattest and most monotonous landscape on Earth. It is covered by sediments—rock, sand, clay, mud, and debris from living things. Most of the sediments near continents originated on land as rock, which was broken down by wind, rain, and ice and whisked downhill by wind, water, and other agents of erosion. When the sediments reached the ocean they continued to slide downward to the deep-ocean floor. Oozes—mushy sediments—blanket about half of the deep-sea floor. They consist mainly of the remains of algae, shells, bones, and teeth and may form a layer more than 1 mile (1.6 kilometers) deep. Only underwater mountains, volcanoes, and deep-sea trenches interrupt the sameness of the abyssal plain terrain.

The conditions on the deep-sea floor—the icy-cold water, inky blackness, and crushing pressure—seem too harsh to support life. At first glance the seafloor resembles a barren wasteland. Yet, the muck teems with life and is one of the richest environments in the sea. It even rivals coral reefs. Most of the animals that dwell on or in the ooze make their living as scavengers. They forage for scraps in the mud or eat "marine snow"—bits of dead organisms and waste material that drift down from higher levels. The rest survive by killing those around them. Most are smaller than a button. Tiny worms, crabs, snails, slugs, brittle stars, and sea spiders are among the most common creatures at these great depths. Despite their distance from the surface, all the residents of the seabed ooze are sustained by sun-dependent food chains. Perhaps the most successful are the sea cucumbers. They strip-mine the ocean bottom, guzzling the ooze and digesting tissue fragments stuck to the mud particles. The filtered mud then passes through their digestive tract and out the other end of their bodies.

A dead humpback whale attracts hungry blue sharks. Eventually what is left of the carcass will sink and provide nourishment for organisms on the sea bottom.

33

Food Chains on Land and Sea

Each species in a food chain depends on the link before it. The typical marine food chain has five links, whereas terrestrial food chains usually have three. On land, plants dominate the ecosystems and can support large grazing animals, such as cows or antelopes. Minute algae predominate in ocean ecosystems. They are eaten primarily by tiny animals, which in turn become meals for bigger animals. Consequently, most large animals in the ocean are carnivores—meat eaters. But on land, herbivores—plant eaters—make up the majority of large animals. Sharks, which are at the top of many food chains, have been described as perfectly designed killing machines. In reality, all predators are perfectly designed killing machines. If they weren't, they would starve.

Most animals eat a variety of food, so ecosystems have food chains complex enough to be called "webs." Humans threaten the balance of many marine food webs by overfishing—harvesting large numbers of favored species. Depleting a species for human consumption may bring the species to the brink of extinction. It also disrupts the complex web of feeding relationships and may cause additional marine species to vanish or others to rapidly increase. Overfishing of a key species, one that many other species depend upon, can trigger the destruction of an entire ecosystem.

Pacific cod, like most predator fish, swallow their prey headfirst to prevent them from escaping.

34

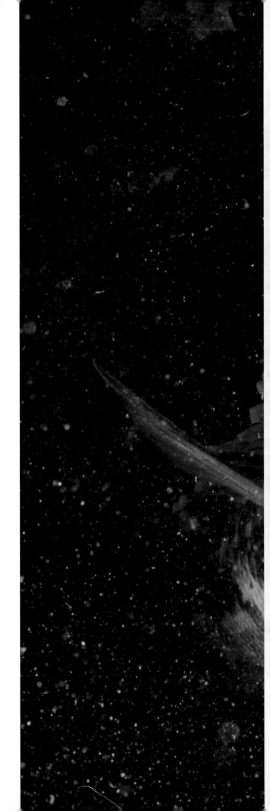

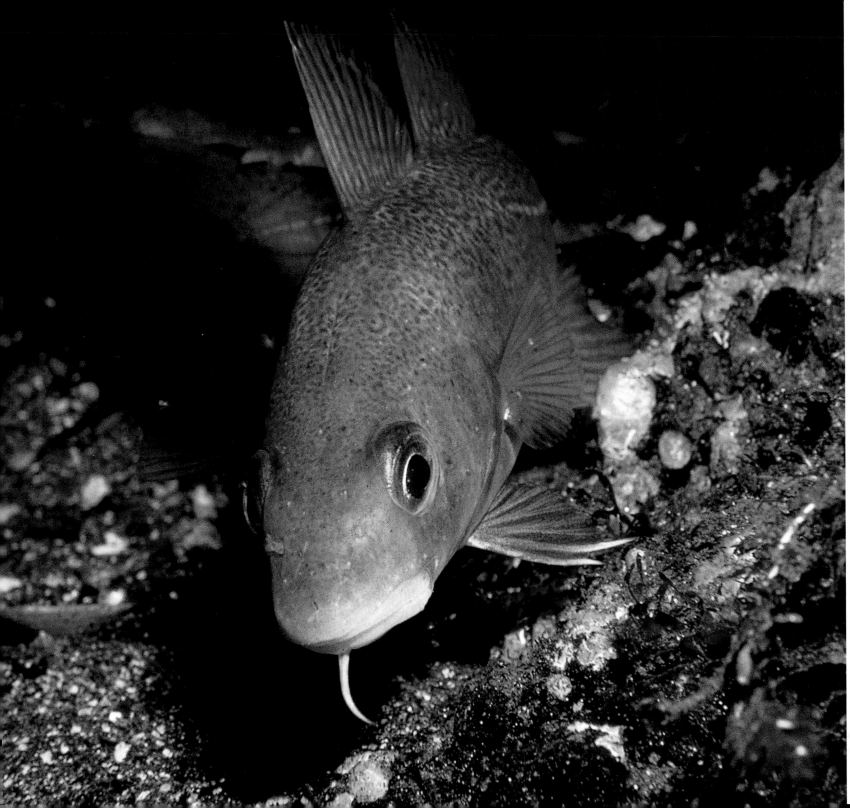

chapter 3

SAFEGUARDING THE NEXT GENERATION

In the Massachusetts State House in Boston hangs a 5-foot-long (1.5-meter) pine carving of a codfish commemorating the importance of the cod-fishing industry to the Massachusetts economy. The bold wooden sculpture bestows nobility upon a fish that is a known cannibal.

Cod are large, homely fish with speckled scales the color of sand or gravel. A lone feeler dangles from a cod's chin like an oversized whisker. Typically, cod grow to be 2 or 3 feet (0.6 or 1 meter) in length. But 100 years ago, cod the size of full-grown men were often pulled from the waters off eastern Canada and the northeastern United States.

Although cod lack the fierce image of sharks, like sharks they are well designed for killing. Cod swim through the water, mouth open wide, constantly prowling for a meal. They are not picky eaters. Cod will dine on anything that they can fit in their mouths and swallow. This includes crabs, shrimp, and clams (shell and all), as well as small schooling fish and even young cod.

Like all fish, cod begin life when a sperm cell from a male fertilizes—unites with—an egg cell from a female. About the size of a small bead, the fertilized egg begins to grow. Cod are "broadcast spawners." During spawning season, each female releases millions of eggs and the males release even greater numbers of sperm. Not all the eggs will be fertilized, and unfertilized eggs cannot develop.

The parents leave their fertilized eggs to the mercy of the environment. Along with other zooplankton, the eggs float at the surface buffeted by wind and currents. Hungry predators feast on the bulk of the eggs before they can hatch. Other eggs may end up in hostile surroundings and perish. The surviving eggs

An Atlantic cod

hatch into tiny larvae within two weeks. Bug-eyed and bulging in front, a cod larva looks nothing like its parents.

Fish larvae may go through one or more stages before becoming an adult. There are exceptions, though; some kinds of fish hatch as miniature versions of their parents. Most fish larvae will be devoured before they can mature. However, since so many eggs are produced, odds are that a few offspring will survive past the larval stage.

Cod larvae have voracious appetites. Starting out with phytoplankton, they feed nonstop and grow big enough within several days to graduate to meals of slightly larger zooplankton. A few weeks later, when the young cod are almost 2 inches (5 centimeters) long, they settle on the rocky seafloor. Here nooks and crannies provide hiding places from other hunters and the young cod can find ample shellfish to eat. If a cod lives to its first birthday, chances are it will reach maturity unless it winds up on a fishing hook.

Emerging from an egg case is a baby swell shark.

Fishers in Alaska bring in their catch of Pacific cod, a species that is much more abundant than its Atlantic counterpart.

Overfishing and the Disappearance of Cod

Running along the shallow Atlantic coast from Newfoundland to New England are immense submerged hills of sand and gravel. Known by names such as the Grand Banks and Georges Bank these drowned hills are to cod what the prairie was to buffalo. Water flowing upward over the banks carries nutrients from the ocean bottom. Near the surface, the nutrients fuel a spectacular growth of phytoplankton. In turn the phytoplankton support directly or indirectly all the animals in the ecosystem from the smallest to the largest. Before Europeans settled in America, cod roamed the banks in vast schools, the fish equivalent of buffalo herds, but in groups numbering in the hundreds of millions.

The cod were free for the taking and spurred a fishing industry that, at its peak, pulled 810,000 tons of cod from Canadian waters in a single year (1968). The cod's downfall was its lean, flaky flesh, which is relatively free of bones and easily preserved by freezing or drying and salting. Although some fish experts wondered if the cod would run out, most others scoffed at the idea. It was widely assumed that cod were so fertile and the ocean so large that the cod would never disappear. After all, one large female cod could lay more than 9 million eggs in a single spawning season.

However, just as the buffalo were nearly wiped out by nineteenth-century hunters, unrelenting fishing over the past 500 years depleted the cod. The fish were caught at a faster rate than they could replace themselves. By the early 1990s fishing nets came up nearly empty. Even though some cod remain in American and Canadian waters, the ecosystem has changed. With the cod nearly gone, lobsters, clams, and other crustaceans now dominate.

PATTERNS OF REPRODUCTION

The ocean is a dangerous world for the young of any ocean animal. The great majority become food for another creature. But each kind of living thing has developed a specific reproductive strategy to ensure that at least a few offspring will live long enough to reach sexual maturity. Generation after generation, species repeat the reproductive patterns that brought them into the world.

Like cod, almost all other bony fish are broadcast spawners. Typically, spawning takes place during spring or early summer. Most fish return to their birthplace to complete this phase of their life cycle. Some make epic journeys to get there. Born in freshwater, salmon spend their adult lives in the ocean and then swim back to their home stream to reproduce and die. The reverse of this migration occurs in eels.

American and European eels are fish but they look like snakes. They spawn in the Sargasso Sea, a large sluggish swatch of ocean near Bermuda, surrounded by the Gulf Stream and the other currents of the North Atlantic Gyre. Huge patches of floating seaweed carpet the surface of the Sargasso Sea. They provide shelter

A European eel

41

for "glass eels," the flat, translucent larvae of eels. The larvae drift with the Gulf Stream for a year or more and develop a thicker and longer body before finding their permanent homes. Then the females enter freshwater streams and rivers in North America and Europe; the males dwell along the coasts. After 5 to 15 years both males and females migrate thousands of miles back to the Sargasso Sea to spawn and die.

Eel Migration and Continental Drift

Continental drift may account for the incredible pilgrimage made by eels. According to the theory of plate tectonics, the Earth's surface is broken into a jigsaw of tectonic plates that move continually, carrying the continents and oceans piggy-back style. In relative motion to each other, the plates collide, pull apart, or jostle past each other. Where plates with continents tear apart, an ocean may eventually develop and fill the gap between them. The North Atlantic emerged where North America split away from Europe more than 100 million years ago.

Eel migration may have started when the newly forming Atlantic was a narrow channel separating the two continents. Seaweed growing in the channel may have provided sufficient food and shelter for baby eels to survive. So, the channel became a breeding site for adult eels living in European and North American waterways, then a short swim away. As the continents drifted apart and the ocean widened, the distance between the spawning ground and the waterways increased by slightly more than an inch (2.5 centimeters) each year. Each generation of eels passed on their migration instinct to the next, spurring on longer and longer journeys. Over millions of years the migration added up to thousands of miles. Today the Sargasso Sea is nearly the size of the continental United States. Encircled by strong currents, it is a calm region of deep and unusually salty water. As in ages past, rafts of sargassum seaweed thrive here, providing an ideal nursery for young eels.

Mr. Mom

Most fish abandon their eggs after spawning, but exceptions occur. In certain species one of the parents—usually the father—safeguards the eggs and protects the juveniles once they hatch. These species produce fewer but larger eggs. Larger

A male ring-eye jawfish expels newly hatched larvae after brooding the eggs in its mouth for a week.

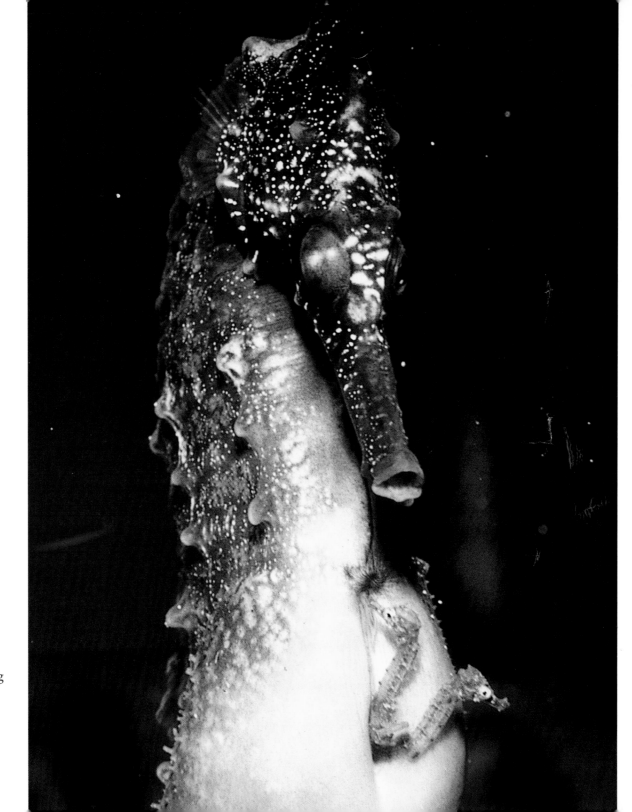

A father sea horse pushes its offspring out of its pouch.

44

eggs result in bigger larvae. They have a better chance than smaller larvae of finding food and avoiding predators. Among these caregivers is the male ocean catfish, who collects the eggs after he fertilizes them. He cradles the eggs in his mouth without swallowing them until they hatch. Afterward, the baby catfish hover near him and flit back to the protection of his mouth when they sense danger.

Male sea horses take parenthood one step further—they actually give birth to their young. The female sea horse places about 200 eggs into a pouch on the belly of the male. The male fertilizes the eggs with his sperm, and the fertilized eggs latch onto the pouch lining. The young sea horses rely on food and oxygen from their father's blood for nourishment during development. A fluid similar to the father's own body fluids surrounds them. Gradually it changes to be more like seawater. As the babies grow, the father's pouch protrudes, like a pregnant woman's belly. The young remain in the pouch for 10 days to 6 weeks, depending on the species. Then the father squeezes them out in a labor that takes up to 2 days. Soon after he finishes, the mother arrives with a new clutch of eggs for his pouch. The males of some sea horse species may carry as many as seven broods of babies during a single breeding season. The young are tiny replicas of the adults and fend for themselves after their birth. While the reproductive strategy of sea horses is effective, the outlook for sea horses is grim. Fishers harvest millions of them each year for use in traditional Asian medicines.

Natural-Born Killers

Sand tiger sharks are born cannibals. They develop from fertilized eggs inside their mother and remain inside her body after they hatch. The young sharks dine on each other and any unhatched eggs. Two juvenile sharks survive this ultimate sibling rivalry, one from each side of their mother's reproductive organ. When they have nothing left to eat they emerge from their mother, seasoned killers with a full set of daggerlike teeth.

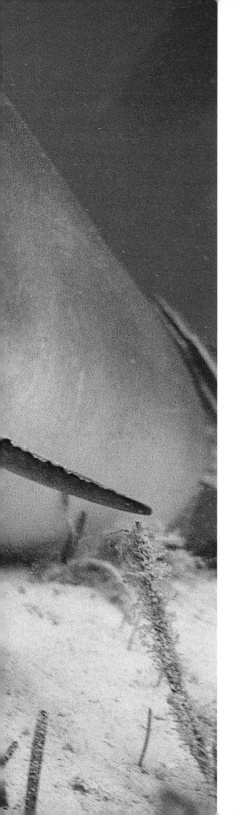

Nearly all kinds of sharks give birth to live young. The males have two special structures—claspers—that let them mate and insert sperm directly into the females. After fertilization a female shark carries a small brood of eggs in a special pouch under the skin until the eggs hatch. Most eggs have enough yolk for the young to develop, but in some shark species the juveniles receive extra nourishment from the body of the mother. Shark babies emerge fully formed and able to care for themselves. A newborn great white shark may measure 4 to 5 feet (1.2 to 1.5 meters) in length and weighs roughly 40 pounds (18 kilograms). Because they are so large, the newborns have an excellent chance of surviving to adulthood.

A Whale of a Mom

Whales invest more time and energy in reproduction than any other marine animal. For example, a female humpback whale carries her unborn calf for 11 months before she gives birth. Newborn humpbacks are enormous, weighing about 1,500 pounds (680 kilograms) and measuring about 14 feet (4 meters), the length of car. Being a mammal, a humpback mother nourishes her baby with milk produced in her mammary glands. The calf guzzles about 120 gallons (450 liters) of milk each day, enough to fill a bathtub. This enables it to gain about 50 pounds (23 kilograms) daily.

Humpback whales are born during winter in warm, tropical seas far from the cold, food-rich polar waters where the adults feed. In the Tropics the waters are calm, making it easier for the babies to learn how to

A lemon shark giving birth

47

breathe. However, there is little for the mother whale to eat. She must live off the energy stored in her blubber. By the time she returns to the feeding grounds she will have lost up to a third of her body weight. She must then store up enough fat during the feeding season to sustain herself and her baby over the next year. When the calf is a year old and doubled in size, it is capable of catching its own food.

Mother whales form strong bonds with their young to keep them near. Consequently, the baby sticks as close to its mother as her own shadow. This prevents the calf from starving and reduces the chance of it being eaten by a shark or killer whale. In the past, whale hunters exploited this bond. They attacked the baby whale first and then the mother when she tried to protect it.

Changing Sex

During a grouper's lifetime it may be both a mother and a father. Groupers are large-mouthed predatory fish that dominate many coral reefs. The lower jaw of some groupers sticks out, giving the fish an ill-tempered and combative appearance. Most groupers begin life as females. After they reach maturity they produce eggs and spawn. When they grow older, female groupers change into males. As a result, nearly all large groupers are male. This transformation is not reversible. Researchers speculate that the transition may be triggered when a female reaches a certain size or if there are not enough males available. Although successful for millennia, this peculiar life cycle is now jeopardizing the long-term survival of groupers. Since fishers prize the largest fish, overfishing can wipe out all the breeding males in a spawning season. Consequently, some types of groupers are already endangered species.

Clown fish are born male but will change sex if given the

These clown fish, known as white-maned anemonefish, live safely among the poisonous tentacles of a sea anemone.

48

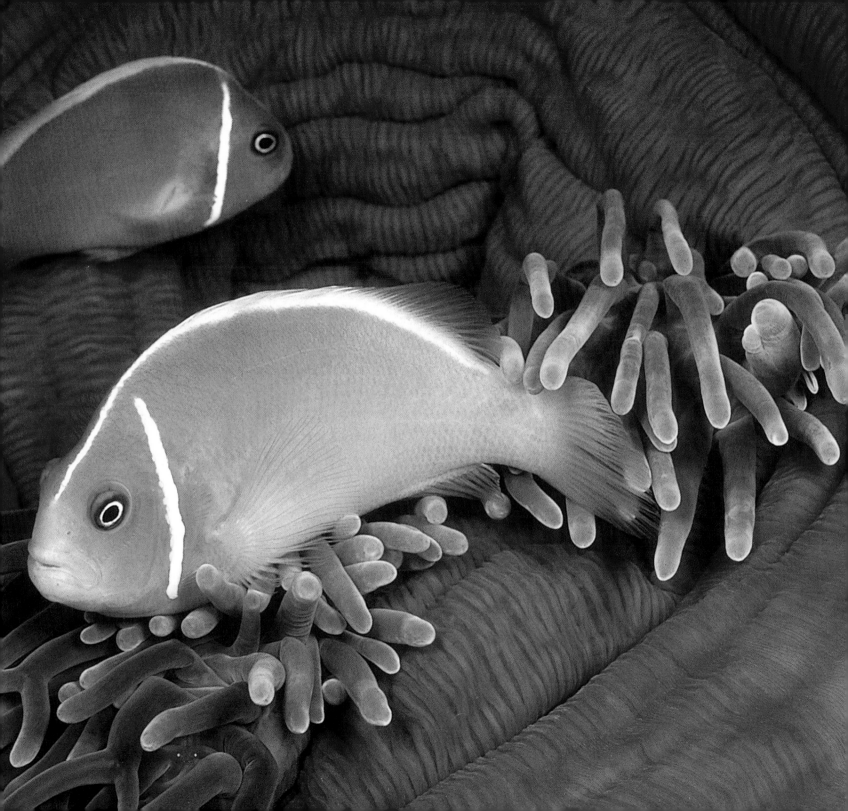

opportunity. They make their home with sea anemones, lower animals that stay in one location for most of their lives. Anemones look like flowers, but their "petals" are actually poisonous tentacles. The clown fish safeguards itself from the deadly sting by covering its scales with a thick, slimy coat of mucous. The clown fish and the anemone live in a mutually beneficial relationship. The anemone protects the clown fish and their eggs from predators. In return, the clown fish remove debris from the anemone and lure fish toward it, providing dinner. Since there is usually space for only two fish within a sea anemone, clown fish are monogamous—limited to one partner. The female clown fish is the larger of the pair. If she dies, her mate mutates into a female and takes a new partner—a small male. This sex change is a one-way street.

However, reef gobies, another kind of fish, are capable of multiple sex changes. If the dominant male in a group of reef gobies dies, the largest female undergoes a sex change to replace him. If a larger male enters the group, the male-turned-female reverts back to being a female.

Sex transformations are not limited to fish. Oysters are male for the first year of life. Then most turn into females for the remainder of their existence.

Having It Both Ways

A sea slug looks like a snail without a shell but with one major difference. A sea slug possesses both male and female sex organs and produces both sperm and eggs. However, a sea slug cannot fertilize its own eggs. To reproduce, it must mate with another sea slug. The sea slugs mate in such a way that they fertilize each other. One kind of sea slug, the sea hare, commonly mates in mating chains, involving four or five animals. The animal at the beginning of the chain acts as a female, and the one at the end acts as a male. All the animals in between perform as both males and females simultaneously.

PROTECTING FUTURE GENERATIONS

Breeding strategies, successful for millions of years, can fail when human hunger and greed upset the balance of nature. White abalone are large shellfish that once thrived off the California coast. Prized for their tasty flesh, they have been harvested to the brink of extinction by commercial and sport fishers. Their recovery is in jeopardy because the remaining abalone are scattered far apart along the ocean floor. Although the females release millions of eggs, a male must be close by when spawning or the eggs and sperm have little chance of mingling.

Many fish and shellfish are taken before they are mature enough to reproduce. Too little is being done to safeguard marine animal populations. Less than 1 percent of the ocean has been set aside for sanctuaries where the harvesting of sea animals is forbidden. Yet, research has shown that where marine sanctuaries exist, fish and shellfish populations have recovered and spread out to the surrounding areas. More sanctuaries are needed.

chapter 4

PURE VENOM

You won't find it advertised in travel brochures but many of the world's most dangerous sea creatures live along Australia's coast. Blue-ringed octopuses, venomous sea snakes, cone shells, stonefish, and sea wasps all pose a lethal threat to unwary swimmers and fishers there. The warm waters off the smallest continent and other parts of the Indian and Pacific Oceans—the so-called Indo-Pacific—are the most deadly in the world. Extending from Africa, past India to Southeast Asia, Indonesia, and Australia, the Indo-Pacific is the site of an escalating arms race between predators and prey. As some animals develop more potent venoms and delivery systems for stunning and killing, their intended victims counterattack with improved defenses and antidotes to neutralize the venom.

Venoms are poisons produced by animals and injected via bites, stings, or puncture wounds. Many contain neurotoxins—toxic chemicals that interfere with the transmission of nerve impulses to the muscles. This disruption results in numbness and paralysis, sometimes followed by death from suffocation (the lungs stop working) or heart failure. Other venoms consist of hemotoxins, toxic chemicals that attack the blood and tissues. They break down capillary walls, producing massive bleeding and swelling. Some venoms combine both neurotoxins and hemotoxins. Many cause excruciating pain.

UNTOUCHABLES: DANGEROUS SEA SNAKES

At least 52 species of venomous sea snakes inhabit the tropical waters of the Indo-Pacific, but none live in the Atlantic Ocean. Sea snakes are air-breathing reptiles with specialized lungs that allow them to remain submerged for at least two hours. Nostrils equipped with watertight flaps prevent seawater from

Eight-armed and dangerous: the pouchlike body of the deadly blue-ringed octopus is about the size of a golf ball.

53

entering. A flattened body with a paddle-shaped tail make sea snakes efficient swimmers. However, most species lack enlarged scales on their belly for gripping the ground, so they cannot slither over dirt and rock like terrestrial snakes.

Sea snakes have smaller mouths and shorter teeth than their land-bound counterparts, but some deliver a neurotoxin at least 10 times more potent than a cobra's. The venom is actually saliva that has evolved to contain a poison. Sea snake bites involving humans usually occur on fishing boats when snakes are hauled up in nets along with the catch. The bite itself is relatively painless and it may take as long as eight hours for symptoms to appear. The symptoms begin with stiff and aching muscles, and may progress to paralysis and then death from the stoppage of breathing. Fortunately, about 75 percent of the bites are "dry"— they lack venom and their victims show no ill effects.

The majority of sea snakes dwell in shallow areas near shore. Dangerous from birth, they dine primarily on eggs, eels, and other fish with slender bodies. Not surprisingly, sea snakes have few enemies except for large fish and seabirds. It has been reported that a sea snake swallowed whole by a fish can bite the inside wall of the fish's stomach and inflict a fatal wound. The snake can then wriggle out of the dead predator's mouth.

MAN-EATING CROCODILES

The saltwater crocodile—made famous by the Peter Pan story—is a reptile that relies on sharp teeth and brute force, not chemical warfare, to subdue its prey. Saltwater crocodiles inhabit wetlands along the tropical coasts of the Indo-Pacific. Their bodies are well suited for life in the water. The scaly skin is water-proof and so tough it can protect against bites of other crocodiles. To swim quickly, a crocodile swings its big tail from side to side. Crocodiles are such accomplished swimmers that they have even been found hunting in waters far out to sea.

Saltwater crocodiles are not fussy eaters. Small ones catch crabs and shrimps. Bigger ones chomp on fish, frogs, turtles, snakes, birds, and small mammals. Although they have dozens of teeth, crocodiles, like sharks, never chew their food. They gulp down small animals whole and rip larger ones into hunks of

A saltwater crocodile

meat. As a crocodile increases in size, so does its ability to grab large mammals. Most kinds of crocodiles rarely attack humans, but saltwater crocodiles are responsible for one of the most gruesome massacres in history.

During World War II, British troops trapped a few hundred Japanese soldiers at the edge of an immense mangrove swamp in Southeast Asia. The swamp separated Ramree Island from the mainland of Burma. Instead of surrendering, the soldiers, including the wounded men, attempted to escape on small boats through the swamp. The swamp was a thick tangle of mangrove trees and home to crocodiles. Attracted by the taste of blood in the water dripping from the wounded, the crocodiles closed in. One by one they picked off the soldiers. In the end, only twenty of the Japanese soldiers were found alive.

Saltwater crocodiles are the largest living reptiles. They may reach a length of 20 feet (6 meters) and a weight of more than 2,200 pounds (1,000 kilograms). An even larger and more ferocious crocodile hunted along the banks of African rivers 110 million years ago. This giant predator was powerful enough to ambush large dinosaurs that came to the water's edge to drink.

Spineless, Slimy, and Deadly

Along many Indo-Pacific beaches, picking up a snail can result in death. Snails are soft-bodied mollusks protected by only one shell. They move by sliding on a single, broad foot. As the foot glides, it oozes a thick slime to make movement easier. The snail's head is at the front of the foot. Snails have a radula, a tongue-like structure attached to the floor of their mouths. In most snails, the radula is covered with miniature, razor-sharp teeth and used like sandpaper to scrape food off surfaces. Some meat-eating snails use their radula to drill through the shells of clams and other hapless victims. Secretions of weak acid from their foot soften the shells and hasten the process. Once the hole is drilled, the snail sucks out the soft meat inside.

Cone shell snails turned their radula into an even deadlier weapon. A lone tooth at the tip of the radula is shaped like a hollow harpoon and functions like a hypodermic needle. It administers a toxin-laced saliva that quickly immobilizes its target. After its first use, the tooth falls out and another replaces it.

A textile cone-shell snail can kill an unwary human with its bite.

56

Cone shells come in three varieties: worm eaters, mollusk eaters, and fish eaters. Fish-eaters present the greatest peril to humans because they have a venom potent enough to stop a moving fish in its tracks. Fish-eating cone shells produce a toxin similar to that of sea snakes.

Octopuses, like snails, are mollusks but they are in a different class and have no external shells. What they lack in protective armor, they make up with brain-power, rivaling fish in intelligence. Octopuses hunt small crabs and other hard-shelled tidbits. An octopus restrains its prey with its muscular, sucker-covered arms and delivers a poisonous bite with a tough, parrot-like beak. To puncture exceptionally hard shells, an octopus may gouge out a hole with its radula. The octopus's venomous saliva paralyzes the prey's body and then turns it to mush, which the octopus sucks.

The bite of most octopuses poses little threat to humans, but the tiny blue-ringed octopus inflicts a venom so powerful that it can kill a person within a couple of hours. Death comes from respiratory failure, and there is no known antidote. Native to the shallow waters of eastern Australia, the blue-ringed octopus prefers sheltered rock pools and crevices. Sometimes it hides inside discarded cans and bottles.

COLOR ME LETHAL: STINGING FISH

The stonefish will not win a beauty contest but it deserves a prize for being the world's most dangerous stinging fish. Stonefish are armed with a row of 13 prickly spines down their backs. Each spine is equipped with two venom glands and grooves to transport the poison. When a person steps on a stonefish, the spines jab far into the foot and the venom squirts deep inside the wound. Within seconds, the unfortunate individual becomes frantic with pain. The agony lasts for hours and may be complicated with breathing difficulty and temporary paralysis. However, the toxin seldom kills. The pain can be relieved slightly by treating the wound with hot water, which breaks down the venom. It may take several months to recover completely.

A stonefish

Stonefish live in the Indo-Pacific. Stings occur when people accidentally disturb a stonefish while wading in shallow water or scuba diving. What makes this fish so hard to recognize is its amazing camouflage. A stonefish's thick, warty skin and brownish-gray coloring blends well with the seafloor. When a stonefish lies perfectly still, it looks like a rock. This disguise allows stonefish to elude predators and ambush prey. They wait motionless for a small fish or crab to stray within striking distance. Then they pounce on the victim and swallow it in one gulp.

Stonefish belong to a family of well-adapted hunters that also includes lionfish and scorpion fish. Their venoms range from mild to deadly and are employed strictly for defense. The lionfish, one of the most beautiful fish in the sea, advertise their toxicity with flamboyant colors, bold stripes, and a brazen display of spines. They do not retreat from danger. Lionfish simply arch their backs and point their spines at an aggressor. Sometimes lionfish work with other lionfish to corral small fish and then take turns eating them. Lionfish live solely in the Indo-Pacific.

The scorpion fish is a master of camouflage. Its red mottled coloring blends in with the algae and rubble on the ocean bottom. Scorpion fish are found not only in the Indo-Pacific, but also along the Atlantic coast from New England to Brazil. However, the venom of Atlantic scorpion fish is less toxic than that of most Indo-Pacific species.

THE KING OF STING

The deadliest creature on Earth, the sea wasp, delivers a sting that can kill a human in less than three minutes. Also known as the box jelly, the sea wasp is a transparent, box-shaped blob of slime about the size of a coconut. A thicket of long, stringy tentacles dangles from the four corners of the main body. Millions of stinging cells—nematocysts—line the tentacles. Each nematocyst consists of a tiny "poison dart"—a coiled, threadlike tube that forms a sharp-pointed barb at the end. When a person brushes against them, the stinging cells fire the darts like a harpoon. The barbs pierce the skin and release the venom.

The venom causes instant, excruciating pain and large purple welts where the tentacles touch. The victim may quickly experience nausea, vomiting, difficulty breathing, and shock. Respiratory paralysis and heart failure rapidly set in and

A lionfish

60

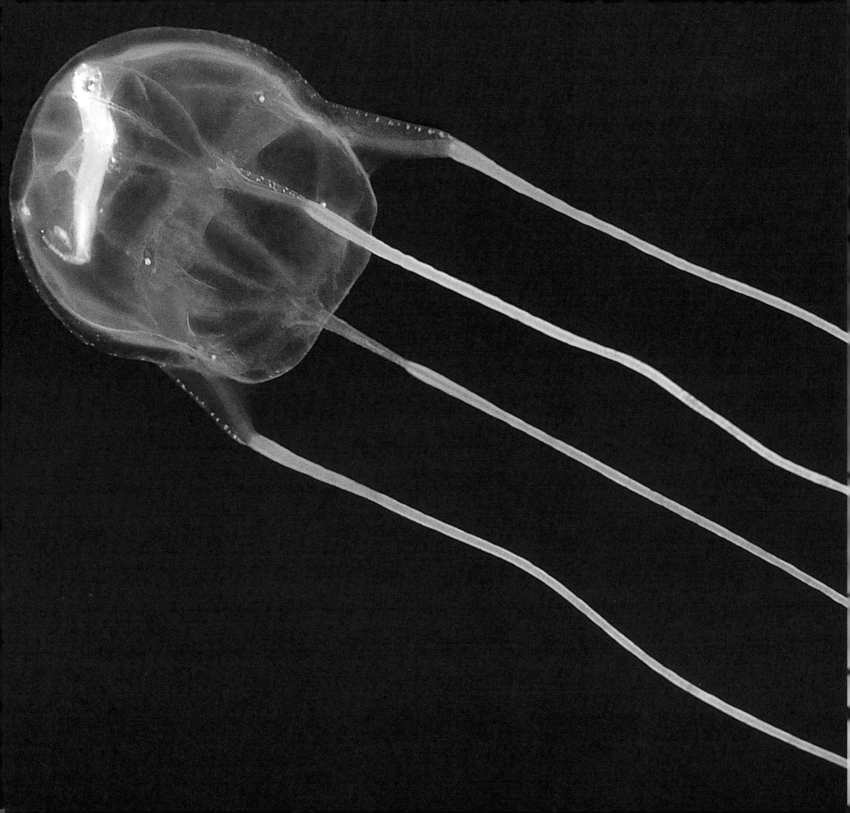

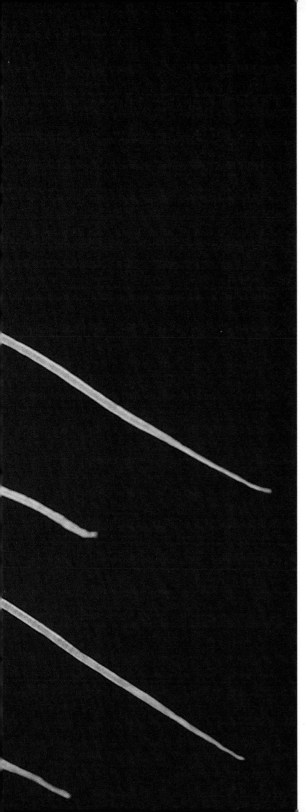

bring on death. However, not all victims die from sea wasp stings. Pouring vinegar over clinging tentacles will prevent them from releasing more toxins. In addition, an antivenin that counteracts the poison is available but must be administered immediately. Wearing a Lycra bodysuit in infested waters provides protection from sea wasp stings as the tiny barbs cannot penetrate it. Wet suits worn by divers provide a thicker shield.

Sea wasps feed on fish and shellfish that they snare in their deadly tresses. A chemical given off by their prey (and unfortunately by human flesh) triggers the stinging cells to fire. The venom evolved to disable quarry instantaneously and avoid a prolonged skirmish. The thrashing of a struggling fish could easily tear the delicate tissues of a sea wasp.

Sea wasps belong to a diverse group of lower animals called cnidaria. All cnidarians are essentially hollow, jellylike sacs with a single opening for slurping in food and water and pushing out wastes. Stinging tentacles surround the opening and serve as weapons.

Cnidarians come in two basic body shapes: tubelike polyps with tentacles pointing upward, such as corals and sea anemones; and umbrella-shaped medusa with tentacles aimed downward, such as medusa jellies and box jellies. Often the tubelike form is permanently attached to one place for most of its life. The umbrella-shaped jellies

A sea wasp with a partially digested fish inside its body

63

The float of a Portuguese man-of-war resembles a fragile blue bubble. It is filled mainly with carbon monoxide gas. To keep the float from drying out, the man-of-war occasionally dips it into the water by tipping sideways.

64

swim freely. They whoosh gracefully through the water by pumping their "umbrellas" open and shut. Medusa jellies are also referred to as jellyfish but they are not fish at all. Real fish are vertebrates; they have backbones. Medusa jellies are invertebrates; they have no backbone.

Of the roughly 200 species of jellies, a mere 70 sting humans. The poisons of most are not lethal to people, although reactions may range from an itchy rash to severe pain. Nematocysts can still discharge after a jelly dies. So caution is always needed when approaching a jelly that has washed up on a beach.

Jellies inhabit all the oceans of the world, and a few kinds make their home in freshwater. Jellies vary in size from the thimble jelly of the Caribbean Sea, which is about an inch (2.5 centimeters) long, to the Arctic's lion's mane, which may grow to 7 feet (2 meters) in diameter. The lion's mane's 200-foot-long (60-meter) tentacles give it the greatest reach of any animal: they can spread over an area the size of a basketball court.

The Portuguese man-of-war, a close relative of medusa jellies, lives at the boundary between air and sea, half in the water, half out. Its blue crest floats above the surface, where it functions like a sail. Its tentacles, which may exceed 100 feet (30 meters), trail in the water, passively fishing for prey. While its neurotoxin is not as potent as that of a sea wasp, it is lethal to most small fish.

A man-of-war is not one organism but a colony of four different kinds of polyps, each with a specialized function. The gas-filled float is a single, specially adapted polyp that keeps the colony afloat. Hunter polyps form the tentacles and catch prey. Other kinds of polyps digest food or carry out reproductive functions.

Portuguese men-of-wars make their home in all the warm seas of the world. Their sting is extremely painful to humans but rarely fatal. To remove any tentacles stuck to the skin, rinse with water but do not apply vinegar as vinegar may make the sting burn more.

Men-of-wars have enemies that are immune to their toxins. Floating sea slugs munch on the tentacles. They swallow the stinging cells intact without harm to themselves. The sea slugs then incorporate the stinging cells into their own tissues and use them for self defense. Sea turtles and ocean sunfish also find Portuguese men-of-wars and other jellies quite appetizing.

CORAL REEFS

Coral reefs are immense undersea "cities" rippling with life. They owe their existence to billions of coral polyps, most of which are about the size of your fingertip. Coral polyps are tube-shaped sacs with a mouth at one end surrounded by stinging tentacles. To protect their soft bodies, corals extract calcium and carbon from seawater to form hard outer shells. They live in large groups, joined together by their shells. When the polyps die, their shells remain in place and new corals construct their homes on top of them. Over thousands of years this process creates mammoth reefs that may extend hundreds of miles.

Corals use their stubby tentacles to stun tiny shrimp and other small animals that drift by. However they cannot pluck enough food from the water to survive. So they supplement their diet with nutrients from single-celled algae that live within their tissues. The algae carry out photosynthesis and provide sugar and starch to the coral. The algae also give the reefs their brilliant coloring.

Reefs come in three varieties. Fringing reefs form closest to the shore, separated from land by a narrow strip of water. Barrier reefs, such as Australia's 1,250-mile-long (2,000-kilometer) Great

Living tapestries, coral reefs are among the richest habitats on Earth.

Barrier Reef, lie farther out and grow much larger. Wide lagoons lie between barrier reefs and land. Atolls are ring-shaped coral islands common in the South Pacific. They originate on top of extinct volcanoes that have sunk beneath the waves. Although rock hard, coral reefs are fragile. They can grow only in clear, shallow, tropical waters and they can survive only within a narrow temperature range.

In the Indo-Pacific, crown-of-thorn sea stars are notorious for eating coral polyps and leaving behind the limestone shells. Periodically they reproduce at such a great rate that their populations explode. Then so many sea stars appear that they cause widespread reef damage. It is not clear whether these outbreaks are part of a natural cycle or if they are caused by human interference with the environment.

Free-floating, fast-growing algae are a perpetual menace to coral reefs as they can overwhelm the reef and prevent sunlight from reaching the guest algae in the polyps. In the past, enormous algae-eating animals, such as parrot fish, manatees, and sea turtles, held algae growth in check. But overfishing of these jumbo-sized grazers upset reef ecosystems. In the twentieth century, sea urchins were the last grazers remaining in significant numbers among the reefs of the Caribbean Sea. The sea urchins successfully curtailed algae growth until the mid-1990s, when disease nearly eradicated them. With sea urchins gone, algae growth went wild, like cancer, choking many of the coral reefs.

More than one-fourth of the world's reefs have been destroyed by human activities. Sewage mucks up the water and blocks sunlight from getting to the coral. Soil and other sediments wash down from adjacent land and smother the polyps. In some places, fishers dynamite reefs or poison them with cyanide to force fish to the surface. One of the greatest threats to reefs comes from global warming—the gradual increase in world temperature caused primarily by the burning of fossil fuels (coal, oil, and natural gas). When tropical seas become too hot, coral bleaching takes place. The polyps expel their algae, losing a vital food source and their coloring. When the water temperature rises too high, the polyps perish.

If the coral disappear, so will many of the sea snakes, blue-ringed octopuses, and other venomous animals dependent on the ecosystem they create. Not even the deadly sting of the sea wasp can protect it from the destruction of its habitat.

Lobe corals are defenseless against a hungry crown-of-thorns sea star.

chapter 5

LIVING ON THE EDGE

One of the most brutal environments on our planet is the intertidal zone. It straddles the narrow expanse of shoreline between the high-tide and low-tide marks. Here, water is tugged relentlessly between land and sea, dancing to ancient rhythms as old as the ocean itself. The edge of the sea changes with the whim of wind-driven waves, the ebb and flow of tides, the advances and retreats of mighty glaciers, and even the rise and fall of shifting crustal plates. What belongs to the land today may be reclaimed by the sea tomorrow.

To survive in the intertidal zone, organisms must cope with pounding surf, abrupt temperature swings, and the stress of living part of the day submerged in water and the other part exposed to the sun and drying air. These harsh conditions are as much the enemy as any hungry predator. Yet, the intertidal zone is awash with nutrients. Each rising tide sweeps in a bounty of plankton and fragments of sea creatures that have died. As a result, a profusion of life carpets this in-between realm. The hardy, often brightly colored inhabitants come equipped with adaptations that allow them to exploit the abundant supply and respond to rapid changes in their surroundings.

The confrontation between land and sea is most evident along rocky coasts. Waves and currents attack unceasingly. They gnaw away at ledges and cliffs, even on calm days. Nature, however, saves its worst for storms when it

Waves batter rocks and the sealife they harbor.

71

unleashes the naked fury of wind and waves. Frenzied seas slam against the coast with enough force to reduce a boat to splinters. Despite the punishment, rugged shores support more life than tamer sand beaches or mudflats because the rocks provide a solid foundation on which living things can anchor themselves. Using strong suction or naturally excreted glues or threads, the organisms cling to rock. They are able to withstand not only the assault of the usual surf but the vicious pummeling meted out by storms.

Marine invertebrates rule here. Instead of a spine, many of these lower animals have rigid outer coverings to protect them from predators, moisture loss, and the crush of wind-whipped waves. Crabs, barnacles, mussels, and sea snails have protective shells. Others, such as sponges, anemones, and sea slugs, have soft, flexible bodies that bend with the movement of water.

The spines of sea urchins provide such an effective defense against predators that sea urchins have few enemies.

73

The Tides

Have you ever set the water in a bathtub in motion and watched it slosh back and forth? If so, you have modeled how tides act in an ocean basin. Along most coasts the level of the ocean rises and falls twice a day. Tides tug on the entire ocean from top to bottom. The force behind them is the gravitational attraction among the Earth, Moon, and Sun.

The Moon's pull on the water is strongest on the side of Earth facing the Moon. The water lifts in a bulge, creating a high tide. At the same time the Moon's pull on the water is weakest on the opposite side of Earth. This water is left behind and creates another bulge and second high tide. Halfway between the two high ones, low tides appear.

As the Earth spins on its axis and the Moon orbits the Earth, the tidal bulges travel also. They remain aligned with the Moon. As the bulges move, the locations they approach experience a rise in water level that gradually becomes a high tide. The process takes about 6 hours, 12 1/2 minutes. Then during the next 6 hours, 12 1/2 minutes as the bulges move away, the water level gradually drops and low tide occurs.

The Sun can make high tides higher and low tides lower. During a full Moon or a new Moon, the Sun and Moon line up with Earth. Together they create an even greater impact on the ocean than the Moon produces alone. Spring tides result. During a spring tide, high tides "spring" to their highest levels, and low tides recede to their lowest. Sometimes the Sun partially counteracts the Moon's influence on the oceans. Small, or neap, tides occur during quarter phases of the Moon, when the Sun pulls at a right angle to the Moon. Then the difference between high tide and low tide decreases. The high tide is not as high and the low tide is not as low. Spring tides and neap tides each occur twice a month.

A half-moon illuminates Brandon Beach on the Oregon coast.

74

SURVIVAL OF THE TOUGHEST

If you observe a rocky coastline at low tide you will see that the inhabitants live in sharply defined horizontal stripes, like residents on different levels of an apartment building. The amount of time exposed to the parching effects of air governs what kinds of organisms can exist at each level.

The splash zone is the highest and driest habitat at the shore. It lies farthest from the sea, usually out of the grasp of waves. Misted by spray, the splash zone floods only during storms or the highest tides. Organisms here must be able to withstand drying out, overheating in hot weather, and freezing in cold. Plantlike blue-green algae eke out a living on the bare rocks. They are so tightly imbedded on rocky surfaces that they appear to belong to the rock itself. Periwinkles—small stocky snails—subsist on the algae. These mini-grazers are to algae what cows are to grass. The periwinkles peel algae off the rocks with their radula. To avoid drying out, a periwinkle retreats into its thick protective shell and seals itself to the rock by spreading mucous along the edge of the shell.

Below the splash zone is a slightly more hospitable landscape, the high-tide zone. Exposed to water only during high tide, it supports limpets, mussels, barnacles, and other animals that can live out of water much of the time. Because these animals are periodically subjected to thrashing waves, they must be able to endure the battering.

Limpets are snails with flat shells. When the tide rises, limpets roam the rocks nibbling on algae. When the tide falls, each limpet returns to its own home spot. This is a scar on a rock that the limpet has carved to perfectly fit its shell. To grip the spot, the limpet creates a powerful suction with its muscular foot.

A mussel is a bivalve—a two-shelled mollusk. When it is young, a mussel produces a mesh of strong, sticky threads to bind itself to a rock. Mussels open their shells during high tide so they can filter out tiny morsels of food from the seawater. When the tide retreats, they shut their shells, locking in moisture. Mussels live tightly packed together on steep-sided slopes.

Barnacles, like mussels, are rock-clinging filter feeders that spread open their shells during high tide. However, the similarity ends there. Barnacles are not mollusks, but crustaceans, relatives of crabs, shrimps, and lobsters. When a barnacle

The rocky shore of Acadia National Park in Maine provides a suitable habitat for these mussels, periwinkles, and rockweed. The mussels and rockweed belong. But periwinkles are not native to the Atlantic coast of North America. They are alien invaders from European shores that may have hitched a ride on ship hulls during the 1800s.

is young, it cements itself to a rock, head down. For better or worse, this place will be its home for life. The barnacle grows a volcano-shaped shell with four plates at the top that control an opening. The part of the barnacle inside the shell looks like a tiny shrimp. To feed, it thrusts its featherlike legs through the opening and combs food particles from the water.

Limpets, mussels, and barnacles cannot protect themselves against carnivores, such as dog whelks and sea stars. Whelks are predatory snails that bore through the hard shells of other animals and feast on the soft parts inside.

The vivacious colors and appealing shapes of sea stars belie their aggressive nature. Sea stars attach suction cups on their undersides to the shells of bivalves. They exert a slow pull until the bivalve's muscles fatigue and its shells open. Then the sea star turns its stomach inside out, and stretches it through its mouth and into the victim's shell. After it digests the prey's delicate tissues, the sea star retracts its stomach.

SPINY-SKINNED ANIMALS

Sea stars are also known as starfish even though they aren't fish. If an arm breaks off a sea star, it can develop into a new individual, while the parent grows a replacement. Sea stars belong to a group of invertebrates known as echinoderms. Echinoderms have hardened spines covering their skin. This group also includes brittle stars, sea urchins, sand dollars, and sea cucumbers. Their external body parts are arranged symmetrically in a circle around a central disk, like spokes on a bicycle wheel. Brittle stars are slender, more fragile relatives of sea stars. Their arms break off easily and can be regenerated. Despite their fragility, brittle stars maneuver quickly to get from one place to another.

Sea urchins look like living pin cushions—spherical with needle-sharp spines. Some tropical species excrete a poison through their spines. Sand dollars have very short spines and look like flattened versions of sea urchins. They live in deeper water, partially buried on the sandy bottom, where they strain plankton from the water.

A sea cucumber is what you would wind up with if you could stretch a sea urchin into a tube and sand down its spines. Most sea cucumbers in the Indo-

Bat stars are a kind of sea star with an appetite for just about any kind of animal they can subdue. This one is devouring a red sea urchin.

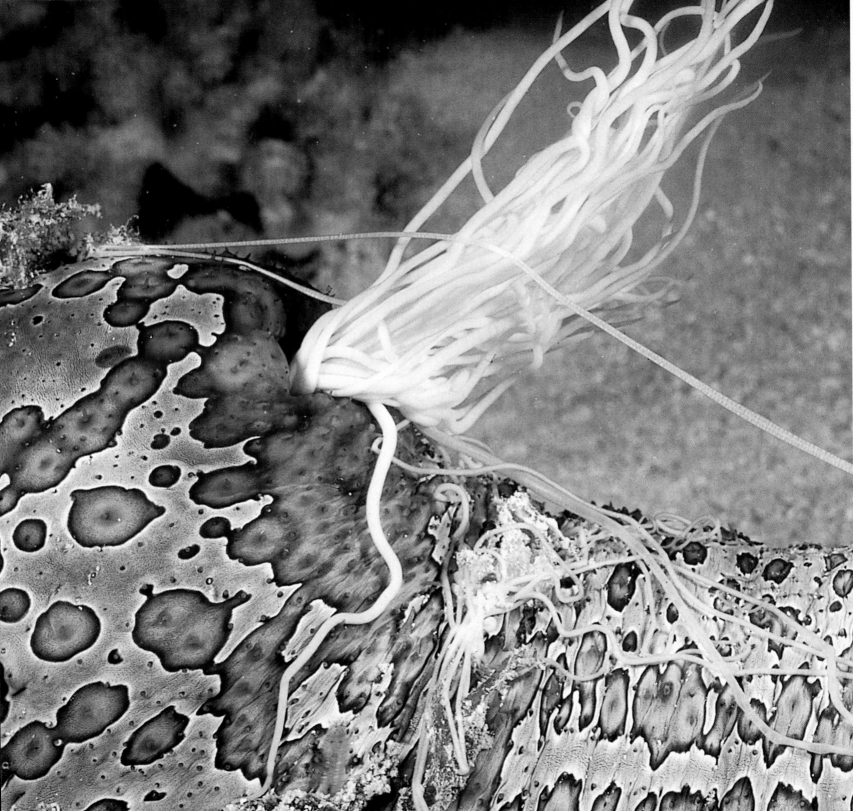

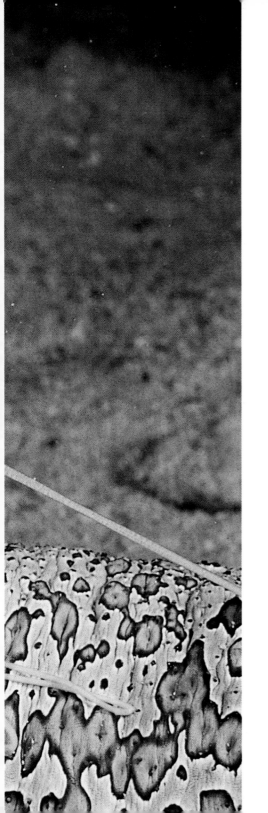

Pacific are poisonous. When one is threatened, it ejects a mass of sticky white threads through its anus, aiming at the attacker. The threads contain a toxin that immobilizes or kills any animal that becomes entangled in them.

Stuck in the Middle: The Mid-Tide Zone

The mid-tide zone is totally covered and uncovered twice a day by water. Its inhabitants must contend with the extreme fluctuations that come with each turn of the tide. Unlike mussels and other rock-gripping creatures, most animals cannot maintain a grasp on the slippery rock open to the surf. Some ride out the extremes wedged in cracks or hidden in pockets under rocks.

Seaweeds—multicellular forms of algae—thrive in the mid-tide zone. Varying tremendously in size, shape, and texture, seaweeds can be big, little, or in-between. They may be round, leafy, tufted, ruffled, flimsy, lacy, or branchlike.

Seaweeds are grouped by color—green, brown, and red. Brown algae can withstand parching better than the others. Red algae prefer moist, shaded areas.

Root-like holdfasts clamp seaweed securely to rocks. On some algae, thick stalks support floppy, leaflike "blades." The largest algae have air bladders—mini-balloons—to buoy them up when the tide comes in and keep their blades separated. When the tide recedes, the seaweed droops over the rocks. It provides a moist refuge beneath its blades for predatory dog whelks and other mobile animals.

To thwart an attacker, this sea cucumber ejects sticky poisonous threads from its anus.

A wider assortment of living things makes a home in the mid-tide zone than in the higher levels. Competition for space is intense, especially in tide pools. Tide pools form when the tide goes out and seawater becomes trapped in hollows in the rocks. The deeper a tide pool and the more water it holds, the greater stability it provides for its inhabitants. Some animals are permanent residents of tide pools, while others ride in and out with the tides. No two tide pools are exactly alike. The ones found along the rocky New England coast differ immensely from those that occur along the coast of the Pacific Northwest or Australia.

Sea anemones, so common on coral reefs, can succeed in many tide pool environments. They latch onto a hard surface with a strong suction and usually remain fixed to one spot. To help retain moisture, anemones live together in colonies shaded by rocks. During high tide, their flexible bodies bend with the flow of waves, reducing the chance of damage. Anemones grope the water with their stinging tentacles, hunting for prey. When the water level drops in a tide pool, anemones tuck their tentacles inside their bodies and coat themselves with slime to keep moisture in.

Sea anemones and sea stars share a tide pool along the coast of Olympic National Park in Washington state.

82

Tapestry of Life: The Low-tide Zone

Water completely engulfs the low-tide zone except during the lowest tides. Life here is easier than in the other zones, resulting in a greater diversity of organisms. Seaweed covers the rocks in thick mats. Large beds of blue mussels abound. Other bivalves, sea slugs, crabs, and worms flourish here too.

Sponges, usually found in deeper water, can tolerate the infrequent dry times. A sponge is a primitive but highly effective water filter. Its body is basically a bag with holes. The body wall consists of two cell layers with a jelly layer sandwiched in-between. Pores—tiny holes—in the outer layer open to admit water. Tiny, whip-like hairs keep the water flowing. The cells in the inner layer strain food and remove oxygen from it. The water then leaves through a central opening in the body, carrying waste products with it.

Sand Beaches and Muddy Shores

Sandy beaches support fewer organisms than rocky shores. Sand bakes in the heat during low tide and provides no hard surface to latch onto. Seaweeds cannot grow here as they would be sucked out by retreating waves. So not only are sea-weeds absent, but the grazers that depend on them have no niche either. Nevertheless, burrowing animals, such as lugworms, cockles, razor clams, and fiddler crabs can find a safe haven during low tide in the moist sand beneath the surface.

Smelly mudflats form where sluggish rivers drain into the sea and dump their load of silt and mud. These muddy shores contain a wealth of nutrients and bacteria. The bacteria release sulfur compounds, which give the mud its distinctive, unpleasant stench. Mud particles clog the breathing apparatus of most shore creatures. Only burrowers with specialized breathing tubes or filters can infiltrate the mud.

In temperate climates, mudflats often transition into salt marshes—wetlands dominated by tall sea grasses. Mudflats and salt marshes provide a happy hunting ground for carnivorous fish and birds. During high tide when water covers the mud, the fish feed on worms and tiny crustaceans. When the tide goes out, hungry wading birds take over.

Many shorebirds are waders. Typically, waders have elongated necks and slender bills to probe mud or shallow water in search of worms and mollusks. They walk on long straight legs with widespread toes that keep them from sinking into the muck. These wading birds on the shore of Sanibel Island, Florida, are being joined by a pelican.

A mudskipper is a
strange kind of fish.
It can "walk" across
mudflats, build
burrows in mud,
and even climb trees.

86

In tropical climates mangrove swamps fringe the shoreline. Mangrove swamps—thickets of salt-tolerant, gnarled, stubby trees—provide a buffer between land and sea. Aboveground prop roots help to anchor the trees and trap sediment, building up the land. Mangroves shield the mainland from the brute force of hurricane waves. Inhospitable to human visitors, mangroves support vast numbers of marine and terrestrial creatures. They also serve as nurseries for countless fish and shellfish destined for human gullets. They even provide a home for mudskippers—fish that can scamper across the slick mud and climb trees using their forefins. Unfortunately, the cutting of mangroves for firewood, lumber, and development threatens mangroves worldwide.

MARINE LIFE BEYOND THE SHORE

The bottom of the low-tide zone merges with the shallow ocean floor rimming the continents. This is a totally marine environment immune from the parching effects of air. In areas protected from waves and currents, submerged fields of sea grass flourish. Strong roots fasten the plants to the seafloor. The flat blades trap sediments and slow much of the water motion, thus stabilizing the sand and the ecosystem. Sea grass serves as a wastewater treatment plant, filtering out contaminants and purifying water.

Like lush meadows on land, dense growths of sea grass provide ample food and places to hide for a large variety of animals. Sea turtles and manatees munch on the underwater grass just as sheep graze in a pasture. Eels, sponges, starfish, conches, and sea urchins forage among the gently waving blades. Like mangrove swamps, sea grass meadows create a nursery for a legion of edible sea animals, including scallops, shrimp, and lobster.

Sea grass habitats are disappearing at a faster rate than tropical rain forests on land. Toxins, nutrient pollution, and disease contribute greatly to their ruin. But overfishing of enormous grazers, such as turtles, is the main culprit. To stay healthy, sea grass must be closely cropped like a carefully tended lawn. Without regular "mowing" by grazers, the blades grow too long, shade themselves, and rot, creating the perfect conditions for mold infestations.

The Future

More than 6 billion people live on planet Earth and each day the population continues to grow. Approximately 60 percent of the global population make their home within 40 miles (60 kilometers) of the sea. As a result, the human demand for food, space, farming, recreation, shipping ports, energy production, and sewage disposal often competes with the needs of sea grass meadows and other ocean ecosystems. Nevertheless, the future of our species is closely bound to the future of the ocean and the life it supports. All living things are part of the same great web of life that links every organism on Earth. Protecting our planet's rich variety of life on land and sea is a major challenge facing humanity.

Glossary

ALGAE—simple plantlike organisms containing chlorophyll but lacking roots, stems, and leaves

BIVALVE—a mollusk with two shells

CNIDARIA—a diverse group of animals that have nematocysts, including box jellies, medusa jellies, sea anemones, and corals

COAST—the zone of land at the edge of the sea where waves are active. Also called the shore.

CONTINENTAL SHELF—shallow sea closest to the continent

CONTINENTAL SLOPE—steep incline separating the continental shelf from the ocean floor

CRUSTACEAN—an invertebrate with jointed legs and a tough outer skeleton, such as a shrimp, lobster, or crab

CURRENT—a broad band of water that flows through the ocean

DECOMPOSER—an organism that feeds on complex chemicals in wastes or dead organisms and breaks them down into simpler chemicals

ECHINODERM—a spiny-skinned invertebrate, such as a sea star or sea urchin, whose external body parts are arranged symmetrically in a circle

ECOSYSTEM—all the living and nonliving things that interact in a specific area

FERTILIZE—the joining together of a sperm and an egg to start the process of growing a new individual

FILTER FEEDER—a marine animal that eats by filtering small food particles from relatively large amounts of water

FOOD CHAIN—the transfer of food energy from one organism to another through predation

GLOBAL WARMING—gradual increase in the average world temperature due primarily to the burning of fossil fuels

GULF STREAM—a powerful, warm surface current that flows along the western edge of the North Atlantic Ocean

GYRE—the horizontal, nearly circular path of water circulation in the open ocean

HEMOTOXIN—a venom that attacks the circulatory system and breaks down tissue

HIGH TIDE—the time when the level of the ocean reaches its highest point

INVERTEBRATE—an animal without a backbone

LOW TIDE—the time when the level of the ocean reaches its lowest point

MAGNETIC FIELD—the area around a magnet in which its force affects objects

MARINE SNOW—the remains of dead organisms and waste material that drizzle down from higher levels of the ocean

MOLLUSK—a soft-bodied invertebrate, usually enclosed in a hard outer shell, such as a clam or snail

NEMATOCYSTS—the specialized stinging cells of jellies, corals, and sea anemones

NEUROTOXIN—a venom that interferes with the transmission of nerve impulses to the muscles

OVERFISHING—the harvesting of a fish species at a rate faster than the species can reproduce and maintain its population size

PHOTOSYNTHESIS—process by which plants and plantlike organisms use light energy to make sugar and release oxygen

PHYTOPLANKTON—microscopic plantlike organisms that use the Sun's energy to manufacture food

PLATE TECTONICS—a scientific theory that explains the movement of continents and the ocean floor

PREDATORS—animals that eat other animals

PREY—animals that are eaten by other animals

RADULA—a tonguelike structure in snails, octopuses, and other mollusks

SALINITY—the amount of dissolved salt in water

SEDIMENTS—small, solid particles that come from rocks or the remains of living things

SHORE—the zone of land at the edge of the sea where waves are active. Also called the coast.

SPAWN—the coordinated release of large numbers of sperm and eggs in water to maximize the chance of fertilization

SPECIES—a distinct kind of individual plant, animal, or other organism

TECTONIC PLATE—one of more than a dozen segments in the Earth's outer shell, called the lithosphere, that move independently

TENTACLES—long, thin, flexible structures surrounding the mouths of jellies, octopuses, and some other kinds of animals; used for grasping, sensing, and in some animals, stinging

Tides—the daily rise and fall of the water in the ocean

Toxin—a poison produced by a living organism

Trench—a deep canyon on the ocean floor

Venom—a toxin transmitted via a bite, sting, or puncture wound

Vertebrate—an animal with a backbone and an internal skeleton

Zooplankton—tiny floating eggs or tiny floating animals, such as shellfish larvae, tiny fish, krill, and copepods

Further Reading

BOOKS

Aaseng, Nathan. *Poisonous Creatures.* New York: Twenty-First Century Books, 1997.

Arnold, Caroline. *Shockers of the Sea and Other Electric Animals.* Watertown, MA: Charlesbridge Publishing, 1999.

D'Vincent, Cynthia. *The Whale Family Book.* New York: North-South Books, 1992.

Goldner, Kathryn A., and Carole G. Vogel. *Humphrey the Wrong-Way Whale.* Minneapolis, MN: Dillon Press, 1987.

Gourley, Catherine. *Sharks! True Stories and Legends.* Brookfield, CT: Millbrook Press, 1996.

Gowell, Elizabeth Tayntor. *Sea Jellies: Rainbows in the Sea.* New York: Franklin Watts, 1993.

Kurlansky, Mark. *The Cod's Tale.* New York: G. P. Putnam's Sons, 2001.

Simon, Seymour. *They Swim the Seas: The Mystery of Animal Migration.* San Diego: Browndeer Press, 1998.

Taylor, Leighton. *Creeps from the Deep.* San Francisco: Chronicle Books, 1997.

WEB SITES

The International Shark Attack File
http://www.flmnh.ufl.edu/fish/Sharks/ISAF/ISAF.htm

Meadows, Robin. "The Green Turtle's Tale." Originally published in *Zoogoer* (Sept./Dec. 1999)
http://www.fonz.org/zoogoer/zg1999/so99turtles.htm

"Seafood Watch" at the Monterey Bay Aquarium can help you make informed choices about which seafood products to buy or avoid in order to support sustainable fisheries.
http://www.mbayaq.org/

Selected Bibliography

BOOKS

Carson, Rachel. *The Edge of the Sea.* Boston: Houghton Mifflin, 1955.

Duxbury, Alyn C., Alison B. Duxbury, and Keith A. Sverdrup. *An Introduction to the World's Oceans.* 6th ed. New York: McGraw Hill, 2000.

Gamlin, Linda. *Secrets of the Sea.* Pleasantville, NY: Reader's Digest Association, 1998.

Hendrickson, Robert. *The Ocean Almanac: Being a Copious Compendium on Sea Creatures, Nautical Lore & Legend, Master Mariners, Naval Disasters, and Myriad Mysteries of the Deep.* New York: Doubleday, 1984.

Hoyt, Erich. *Creatures of the Deep: In Search of the Sea's "Monsters" and the World They Live In.* Buffalo, NY: Firefly Books, 2001.

Kingsland, Rosemary. *Savage Seas.* New York: TV Books, 1999.

Nybakken, James W. *Marine Biology: An Ecological Approach.* 5th ed. San Francisco: Addison Wesley Longman, 2001.

Payne, Roger. *Among Whales.* New York: Dell Publishing, 1995.

Praeger, Ellen J., with Sylvia A. Earle. *The Oceans.* New York: McGraw-Hill, 2000.

Snyderman, Marty, and Clay Wiseman. *Guide to Marine Life: Caribbean, Bahamas, Florida.* New York: Aqua Quest Publications, 1996.

MAGAZINE AND NEWSPAPER ARTICLES

Broad, William J. "Evidence Puts Dolphins in New Light, As Killers." *New York Times,* July 6, 1999.

Kunzig, Robert. "Twilight of the Cod." *Discover,* April 1995, pp. 44-58.

Web Sites

"Shark attack in the Gulf of Aqaba" by O. Goffman and Kari Lavalli, Israel Marine Mammal Research & Assistance Center Web site

http://maritime.haifa.ac.il/cms/immrac/research/sharks.htm

"Undertakers of the Deep" by Cheryl Lyn Dybas. *Natural History,* November 1999 online

http://www.amnh.org/naturalhistory/features/november99_whales.html

About the Author

Award-winning author Carole Garbuny Vogel loves the ocean and lives 90 minutes from the beach. Her favorite water sport is boogie boarding, which is a lot like surfing but instead of standing up on the board, she lies flat. On beach days when the waves are small, Carole enjoys reading a good book or strolling on the sand looking for shells.

On workdays, Carole Vogel can usually be found "chained" to her computer, wrestling with words. She specializes in high-interest nonfiction topics for young people. Among her many books are *Nature's Fury: Eyewitness Reports of Natural Disasters* (winner of the Boston Authors Club Book of the Year Award), *Legends of Landforms: Native American Lore and the Geology of the Land* (an NCSS/CBC Notable Social Studies Trade Book), and *Shock Waves Through Los Angeles: The Northridge Earthquake* (placed on the Children's Literature Choice List). Carole Vogel is the coauthor of *The Great Yellowstone Fire,* which was named one of the 100 Best Children's Books of the Century by *The Boston Parents' Paper.*

Carole Vogel's books have been chosen for many reading lists, including Outstanding Science Trade Books by the NSTA-CBC, Best Children's Books of the Year by the Children's Book Committee at Bank Street College of Education, and the Science Books & Films' Best Books for Junior High and High School.

A native Pennsylvanian, Carole Vogel grew up in Pittsburgh and graduated from Kenyon College in Gambier, Ohio, with a B.A. in biology. She received an M.A.T. in elementary education from the University of Pittsburgh and taught for five years before becoming a science editor and author. She keeps in touch with her readership by giving author presentations in schools and libraries.

Carole and her husband, Mark, live in Lexington, Massachusetts, where they enjoy frequent visits from their two children, who recently graduated from college. You can learn more about Carole Vogel at her Web site: *http://www.recognitionscience.com/cgv/*